D0129267

INTENTION HEALS

A Guide and Workbook

ADAM

Author of DreamHealer Books and DVD

Additional copies can be purchased at:
www.dreamhealer.com

Copyright © 2008 by DreamHealer Inc.
All rights reserved.

Published in 2008 by DreamHealer Inc.
Canadian Cataloging in Publication Data
ISBN 978-0-9732748-5-1
UPC 798304009637

Adam, 2008, Intention Heals - A Guide and Workbook
Printed and bound in Canada.
First Printing - August, 2008
All rights reserved.
No part of this publication may be reproduced, stored in an electronic database or
transmitted in any form by any means — electronic, photocopying, recording or otherwise,
— without the prior written permission of the copyright holder.

The information contained in this book is not intended to be used for diagnosis or treatment
of any health disorder whatsoever. It is not intended to replace consultation with your
healthcare professional. See your physician if you have a medical condition. The author
and publisher are not liable for the misuse of the material in this book.

Cover design by: Emmarose Louise Gallant
Edited by: Dr. Doris Lora

Mixed Sources
Product group from well-managed
forests, and recycled wood or fibre
www.fsc.org Cert no. SW-COC-1271
© 1996 Forest Stewardship Council

Acknowledgements

I want to thank Dr. Bruce Lipton, Dr. Lee Pulos, Dr. Heather Fay, Dr. Edgar Mitchell and Dr. Warren Bell for their inspiration and words of wisdom. Thanks to Dr. Doris Lora, my editor and Ivan Rados, artist, for their help in creating this useful guide and workbook. I especially want to thank my parents, Frank and Liz, for their dedication, and my sister, Sarah, for her help from time to time. Also many thanks to my grandparents, Ken and Doris, for their enthusiasm and support of my work. And a special thanks to those who have read my books, attended my workshops and shared freely of themselves in their survey responses and testimonials to help others.

Also by Adam

Books

DreamHealer- A True Story of Miracle Healing (Canada/USA)

*DreamHealer- A Guide to Healing and
Self-Empowerment (Canada)
OR
The Emerging DreamHealer- A Guide to Healing and
Self-Empowerment (USA)*

The Path of the DreamHealer (Canada/USA)

DVD

DVD- Visualizations for Self-Empowerment

*Registration for Intention Heals (DreamHealer)
workshops, purchase of DVDs and books are available at
www.dreamhealer.com*

Books are also available at your local bookstore.

*Stay in touch by signing up for my free newsletter at
www.dreamhealer.com*

Table of Contents

Introduction

"The power of imagination makes us infinite."
- John Muir

I am 15 years old. I am watching TV in the family room with my dad and sister. Suddenly the familiar, wrenching sound of muffled screams comes from upstairs. Mom is having another severe pain attack as one of her multiple sclerosis symptoms, trigeminal neuralgia, kicks into high gear.

As if moved by an invisible force, I stand up and walk to the foot of the stairs. I hesitate and then as if gently nudged, find myself climbing up the stairs and entering into the room where my mother is lying in bed, clutching a pillow to her face to muffle screams of pain.

I walk over to her and place my hands on her head. "Close your eyes, Mom," I say, not knowing why I am doing this. I go into a very deep trance and I can't see anything around me except images of my mom in front of me. I find myself navigating throughout her head. I see a green pulsing light and it is obvious to me that this is where the problem is. I grab it and pull it out of her.

That was six years ago and she has not had another attack since. My energetic intention to relieve the suffering of my mother, combined with her wish to be well, brought this impressive result. Our minds were joined in this common intention, apparently facilitated by a natural ability I had been given to focus my energy toward a specific goal.

This was the beginning of an amazing journey I could not have predicted. I have been privileged to join with thousands of people in facilitating their self-healing abilities as we jointly focus our energies in this single intention.

A Brief History

This book you hold in your hands, *"Intention Heals,"* is my fourth book in the "DreamHealer" series motivated by my conviction that, with a few simple tools, we can all learn to help ourselves heal.

For the last six years I have been drawn to healing and helping others achieve self-empowerment through exploring the use of their own innate energy resources. In 2003, I wrote my first book, *"DreamHealer,"* to share my healing gift, with the intention of encouraging others to more comfortably express their unusual experiences and gifts openly. In it, I chronicle my healing discoveries, including distant healing and the basic principals of quantum physics as they relate to healing. The publicity surrounding the release of *"DreamHealer,"* sparked an enormous interest, along with an overwhelming number of requests for healing. I saw first-hand the desperate need for healing of body, mind and spirit.

Not knowing how to respond to such a demand, I was thrilled to discover that my healing abilities were effective with groups as well as individuals. I could merge the auras of a group of participants into one coherent frequency to effectively hold group healings which I have done for several years. Group treatments, I discovered, provide an energetic jump-start to one's healing.

I also discovered that visualizations are powerful tools we can use to create our reality by using our intentions. To teach these tools, I wrote my second book, *"DreamHealer – A Guide to Self-Empowerment."* My DVD, *"Visualizations for Self-Empowerment,"* provides graphic visualizations, bringing them to life with colorful animation and narration.

I soon realized that people were asking for more tools and more explanations as they experienced paradigm shifts and explored new beliefs about self-empowerment. So in my third book, *"The Path of the DreamHealer,"* I connected the dots between our experienced reality and our actual inter-connectivity and discussed its combined impact on our own physical, mental and spiritual health.

As I interact with the thousands of people who come to my workshops and listen to their questions, my understanding grows and my work expands. I continue to merge the latest cutting edge science with the mystical traditions of my aboriginal forefathers. I have embraced this wisdom about subtle energies, as I blend it with the channeled insights I've received about distant energy healing. I am very excited to be able to combine these insights with the most recent scientific information from molecular biology, my major at University.

This fourth book, "*Intention Heals*", is the culmination of years of facilitating individual and group healings, presenting healing workshops and conferences and discovering scientific data which support my intuitive knowledge. At my workshops, I explain the relationship between science and my intuitive or channeled information about energy healing. Then I facilitate unique group healings where auras of all participants are merged into a coherent resonance. Individuals are then guided step by step in their own self-work within the context of the group. The entire gathering resonates as an ordered energy, creating the ideal conditions to amplify healing intentions. I have received thousands of testimonials of amazing changes occurring in people's health following these group energy treatments.

Intention Heals Survey

The evidence that "*Intention Heals*" is impressive! Over the past several years there has been an on-line survey for participants who have read the "*DreamHealer*" books and/or have attended "*Intention Heals*" or "*DreamHealer*" workshops and practiced these techniques. With over 2,500 registered replies, the results are remarkable! Over 75% of respondents rate their health issues as having improved significantly through these self-empowering practices. A few of the overwhelming number of testimonials are in the last section of this book.

Survey Participants Summary

Intention Heals Questions	Answers	
	Yes	No
Have you read any of the DreamHealer books?	93.02%	9.58%
Have you been to a DreamHealer workshop?	43.80%	55.13%
Do you do healing visualizations as recommended by DreamHealer?	76.79%	21.90%
Do you feel that your health has improved as a result of the books or workshops?	75.79%	22.42%
Is your primary health concern gone?	29.00%	68.65%

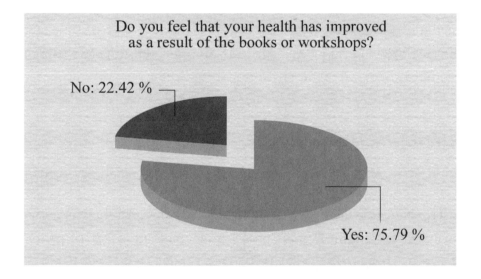

Do you feel that your health has improved as a result of the books or workshops?

No: 22.42 %

Yes: 75.79 %

Using Chi-square and binomial statistical testing (analysis by Statistics Made Easy, Inc), results show that a statistically significant number of people reading DreamHealer book(s) and/or attending DreamHealer workshop(s) :

1. ***Do healing visualizations***
2. ***Experience health improvements***
3. ***Nearly a third no longer have their primary health concern.***

The bottom line is that people are taking control of their own health challenges and making a difference.

In addition to my own workshops, I have had the honor of presenting my material about intentional healing jointly with several of the most forward thinkers in this field. During 2006, a series of conferences entitled *"**Intention Heals**"* were held throughout North America with Dr. Edgar Mitchell, astronaut, author and founder of the Institute of Noetic Sciences (IONS); Dr. Bruce Lipton, cell microbiologist, author and researcher; Dr. Lee Pulos, author and clinical psychologist and myself. It was an amazing experience to combine and integrate cutting edge quantum physics, the latest research in biology and the psychology of consciousness with group energy sessions.

These conferences provided participants with what they needed to know in order to activate healing through self-empowerment triggered by our primary catalyst: intention. This collaboration also fueled my quest for knowledge. I have felt increasingly compelled to anchor my innate gifts and subtle energy sensitivities in a framework of breakthrough science which I have found in the study of molecular biology.

I have also had the pleasure of working with people from various complementary healing modalities such as Qi Gong masters,

Reiki masters and shamans from many indigenous cultures as well as people who have discovered these abilities on their own. Every healer has learned slightly different ways to access their ability. What I have learned is that each and every one of us naturally possesses this healing capacity. We just need some simple directions as to how to maximize our awareness of it and focus our intentions to guide it.

My First Nations (Native American) cultural roots have had a very profound influence on my work. I have had the privilege of participating as an invited healer in many sacred healing rituals which have shaped my approach to energy healing. The elders, shamans and others have taught me many things about aboriginal culture, ceremonies and way of life.

During one such private healing ceremony, the eldest shaman held the speaking staff and opened the ceremony with his blessings. Then to my surprise, I was passed the speaking staff as I was the youngest healer present. I thanked them for inviting me into the sacred ceremony and expressed my intention to work toward self-empowerment of our people. Knowing that I was privileged to participate in the same ceremony that had taken place over thousands of years was an awesome experience. I thought of my Great-Great-Great Grandpa Sockalexis who was a shaman for his people and how he would have participated in an identical ceremony many years before. What amazing spiritual growth I experienced as I was healing side by side with shamans who had gathered from throughout the world!

This ancient wisdom is becoming more main-stream. It is encouraging to see that more medical doctors are becoming aware of the importance of a holistic view of medicine. Dr. Mehmet Oz, a well-known cardiovascular surgeon who often appears on the "Oprah" show stated, ***As we get better at understanding how little we know about the body, we begin to realize that the next big frontier in medicine is energy medicine. It's not the mechanistic part of the joints moving. It's not the chemistry of our body. It's understanding for the first time how energy influences how we feel.***"

Now, in my fourth book, I continue this theme of joining science and ancient wisdom as our awareness moves toward the goal of the scientist and mystic being of one mind. The logic is simple. Our thoughts are energy. Intention is focused thought which affects all physical matter. Once you decide to take control of your mind which in turn regulates your body, then you will be in control. To assist you in taking control, I continue to refine and teach practical self-healing exercises backed up by my experience and by current scientific discoveries.

My studies at University have shown me what science is beginning to discover about the biological and chemical correlates of our thoughts and intentions. The carrier or dynamic at work is energy. The beauty of self-empowerment is that you are making this discovery yourself, as you learn to activate and maximize your own innate energy abilities to create your reality of health and well-being.

Introduction

Self-healing knowledge resonates not only in your energetic field but in everyone's consciousness that you have ever been connected to in thought, word or deed. As we access this ability, it is amplified through our inter-connectedness. In doing so you are not only helping yourself, you are helping the entire planet.

The first section of *"Intention Heals"* summarizes my experiences and provides an overview of the science behind intentional healing. A brief technical discussion of your vital mind-body connection is essential for a deeper understanding of the external and internal influences that shape your emotions and belief system.

The next section consists of a workbook in two parts. Workbook Section I has step-by-step methods of examining and changing your perception of events. You will learn how to create a more optimistic reality. These exercises will prepare you for the more specific techniques that follow.

Workbook Section II contains the visualization exercises, where you will learn with confidence how to customize visualizations for your particular wellness goals, or other achievements. Learn to trust the process of allowing *your own* creative guidance to lead you. Experience self-empowerment as you transform your reality with the power of your intentions.

In the final section are submissions from readers and workshop participants which provide helpful ideas about how others customize their visualizations for wellness.

My Journey

"The mystical is not how the world is but that it is."
- Ludwig Wittgenstein

Growing up I had a relatively normal urban childhood. My family was not into energy healing and we didn't talk about auras or anything like that. This simply never came up in conversation. But I always saw auras, the subtle energy surrounding all living organisms. Thinking this was normal, I assumed that everyone experienced this, so I never mentioned it. When I was 13 years old, strange telekinetic events started happening, like pencils and erasers flying out of my hands. But it wasn't until my family witnessed some of these telekinetic episodes that we all began to think something unusual was going on. Then, as described in the introduction, during my first healing experience, I facilitated my mother's healing of trigeminal pain.

My parents spent many sleepless nights trying to figure out what was happening. Dad would bring people home from his work and I would tell them what I saw regarding their health issues or do treatments with them. By word of mouth, news spread about my healing abilities.

Then I had a healing experience which launched me into the public eye. When I was 16, I read a newspaper story about Ronnie

Hawkins, a famous Canadian rock 'n roll musician and his diagnosis of terminal pancreatic cancer. The article reported that surgery, chemotherapy and radiation were not options for him and his doctors told him he had only two to three months to live. This story gripped me and I had a strong intuitive awareness that I could help him. So I emailed and asked him if he'd be willing to let me work with him. Having nothing to lose, he agreed.

From 3,000 miles away, I began the treatments. I instructed him to lie down at 7 o'clock and let me know what he felt. At 7 o'clock when I did the treatment (focusing my intentions on destroying the tumor), he felt a pulsing in his stomach. It was very obvious to him that there was a strong connection happening between us.

Ronnie knew that these distant energy treatments were working. I continued the treatments for several months. Ronnie got another CT scan and an MRI and the doctors all concluded that there was no sign of cancer. The tumor was completely gone. As I write this in 2008, he has had six more birthdays and he is still cancer-free. As Ronnie said on the **Health-on-the-Line** TV show in 2003, "I think Adam is for real. I think he's got something special. It's a miracle as far as I'm concerned."

News travelled about Ronnie's recovery, including an article in "**Rolling Stone**" magazine, followed by many TV and radio interviews, as well as magazine and newspaper articles from all over the world. Around this time I met former astronaut Dr. Edgar Mitchell, who became my early science mentor.

What I Experience When Healing

Many times I have been asked what I experience when I conduct a healing. It is difficult to explain what I "see" when I refer to an image in healing. This "seeing" is an awareness or feeling of knowing, more than sensing in any ordinary terms. I pick up information and my brain deciphers it by putting it into a form I can relate to. For instance, if I am looking at a tumor, the collection of information comes through as a three-dimensional live view of the tumor in my mind.

Healing is accomplished through various types of connections. In distant healing, a person's photograph allows me to connect by serving as a guide to get to that specific frequency which is unique to that person. Healing in person provides a similar identification of frequencies to accomplish the healing exchange of information. In group healings, I merge the auras of all participants into a coherent frequency, allowing the entire group to resonate together.

When healing, I feel/see images of interacting, vibrating frequencies connecting to a web or network of frequencies. Everyone has a unique frequency within this web of interconnectivity. I focus to reach a coherent energy frequency by altering mine, in order to get closer to the unique frequency of the person I am healing. This synchronization of frequencies occurs quickly. I do not know why or how I am able to make this connection so easily. A more in-tune resonance results in more complete information being exchanged. During this time, I am able to pick up information about the person's past, present and future self, including health issues. Using my intentions, I then transfer the information to them which they need so they can manifest positive health changes. This works most effectively if the person's (healee's) intention for better health is aligned with the healer's intentions.

I am less attached to my physical self during this process but am never totally disconnected from self. This is because I am not resonating at another person's identical frequency but close enough to cause an influence on the person. My state could be described as a dissociated state of total awareness. Altering my own frequency is the mechanism that allows a smooth connection of information between the transmitter (healer) and receiver (healee) of health information.

At the point where the frequencies are closest, they resonate with each other, allowing me to receive information about the person and their beliefs, including whether they are ready to receive incoming messages and change accordingly. The healer/healee continue resonating together, exchanging quantum information in this "pinging" fashion.

There are a great number of variables as to how a person responds to this process. These include their beliefs, attitudes, relationships with self and others and intentions. The connections are always more focused, powerful and intense when the intentions are similarly focused between the healer and the healee. Although the intentions of others affect your health, your own intentions far outweigh the intentions of those around you. Your intentions are a combination of your fears, beliefs, doubts, expectations and your will to live. Other people's thoughts only affect you as you allow them to.

Intention requires synchronizing conscious and subconscious

thought patterns in order to invoke change. Visualizations provide conscious focus and if they are fueled by emotional impact, they are more powerful and can be easily aligned with subconscious thought. This is the focus of "***Intention Heals***" as I am able to "see" how visualizations positively influence health issues. Healing is an innate ability which can be enhanced by various teachable techniques and practices. Have the greatest respect for your own ability to heal yourself and know that visualizations are an effective way to focus your intentions on healing.

A Brief Science Tutorial

Being a scientifically minded person, I have been drawn to academia to search for answers. I want to understand what is happening physiologically with energy healing through intention.

Several years ago when I first started University, I floundered as I didn't find any information that inspired me. Then in my second year, I discovered the field of molecular biology which is the study of the structure and function of biological molecules. I became totally captivated. This new field encompasses ground-breaking research on the molecular interactions in DNA and proteins that drive life itself. Their behaviors and interactions seem to indicate an awareness as they "respond," "behave" and "react" to environmental triggers.

Let me share some very interesting insights from molecular biology as to how intention can play a role in healing. If you find the following scientific information too complex, just keep in mind the most basic and most important point: life and healing are dynamic (constantly changing, rather than static) – which means that there are infinite potential outcomes. And YOU can influence those outcomes.

The central scientific questions for me are:
(1) How do our intentions affect our metabolism?
(2) How do such intentions directly activate metabolism to
*   heal ourselves most efficiently and effectively?*

During my studies I have been fascinated by the dynamic nature of all molecules of life. What we see in a text book is a diagram of a static protein structure, yet the actual structure of a protein is far more complex, due to its dynamic nature. At present, scientists in molecular biology crystallize proteins to examine the static view of their structure. This process of freezing them in time is called crystallography which provides us with a snap-shot view of a protein. We know they are moving and are very conformationally dynamic but the only way we can get a picture is when we force one at a time to stay in one conformation.

As proteins are dynamic in nature, they are constantly changing their conformations. Certain conformations enhance the rate of a reaction more than others which we describe as being more enzymatically active. Here's the important part. This means that just the smallest change in structure or orientation of any part of this protein has dramatic effects on its enzymatic activity and, consequently, our health. Metabolism is based on enzyme (which is a protein) activity and these enzymes are directly influenced by our intentions and thoughts.

You can now appreciate that there is no such thing as an idle or neutral thought. This should be a huge motivation for you to practice positive thoughts.

Specifically, just how are proteins chemically changed by intentions? Every time we think a thought, many chemical reactions occur and every chemical reaction emits light. This has been known for decades. In fact, we use this light-emitting feature to identify a substance by running light through it and observing which light frequencies it absorbs and which light it emits. So a thought actually becomes a "light-emitter."

Now we are getting to the crux of the matter: this light our thoughts have emitted directly affects the conformations of the proteins in our bodies. Biologists have become aware that even small amounts of light cause alterations in protein orientation and conformation. This has direct effects on the conformation of the entire enzyme.

To summarize, our thoughts and intentions are constantly emitting light and this light directly influences protein conformations. Everything goes back to those very important thoughts and intentions. With our current scientific technology, it is very difficult to observe this in the lab, especially for large proteins. This is because the only way we can analyze the proteins in good resolution is in a static view by crystallography. However, it is clear that light influences large protein conformations, though we cannot observe this yet. This will be a focus of my research and I have started working in a structural biochemistry lab where I intend to get further insights into this research.

How much does current science really understand about your metabolism? We are a long way from knowing everything about metabolism, or what's going on in the body at the molecular level of interactions. As an example, the following image is called an interactome. Every dot represents an enzyme or a protein. Every line represents an interaction between these proteins and, as you can see, there are a lot of interactions that are very complex. But just because there's a dot there doesn't mean we know what that interaction is and how it works. The majority of these interactions have not been directly proved but are assumed to interact.

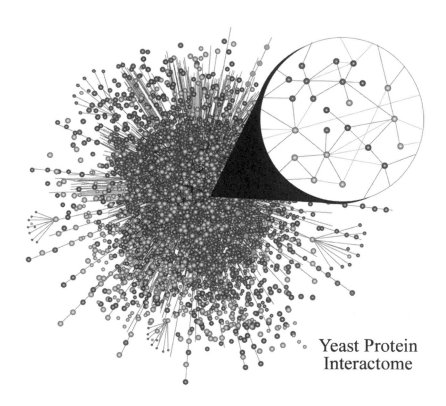

Yeast Protein
Interactome

The interactome shown is of a yeast, a simple organism in comparison to a multi-cellular organism, such as ourselves. I show it because of its simplicity compared to a human interactome. But you can see that it's actually not that simple. There are some very complex interactions happening here that we know very little about and these are just the known proteins and the known interactions between these proteins. The way scientists determine whether an interaction exists is really quite crude. After disabling one protein, scientists note which proteins are affected, thus indicating a codependence or interaction between the two proteins.

So, why am I showing you this interactome? One of the core scientific concepts that I agree with intellectually and intuitively is homeostasis, or the constant balancing of the body's systems for optimal health.

Maintaining homeostasis maintains health. All of your biochemical systems are constantly adjusting and reacting to new information because your body is flexible and dynamic at the cellular level. Sometimes it is difficult to visualize how a problem could be corrected because someone may have used the word "incurable." This could be more accurately stated that we currently don't understand "how" your body could balance itself – how it could return to homeostasis given your symptoms. This does not mean that your body does not have a mechanism to resolve the issue.

Imagine, as you look at the image of an interactome, that if you damage any enzyme in that cell, there are a multitude of alternate enzymes ready to take its place. All of these interactions and all of these proteins are designed to maintain homeostasis; to maintain balanced health within the cell. That's what these interactions are for; to compensate for each other. In your body there are countless such mechanisms to compensate for your health imbalance.

By stimulating one group of proteins to make up for the lack of another, your body minimizes the problems of that dysfunctional part. That's the point of showing this interactome. Our innate life force has many brilliant ways to compensate for whatever the problem is. Whether you understand the complexity or not, you can always visualize every cell helping to restore the functioning of any gland or organ. Know that your body always has another mechanism to deal with any problem.

Once again, regardless of how much is known or how complex a process is, all of us can reach a basic understanding of how metabolism works. From there, we can visualize in greater detail how to mentally manipulate metabolism to facilitate the healing process.

Dr. Bruce Lipton, cell biologist, is a pioneer in the field of epigenetics, a relatively new field which deals with how the environment influences our genes and how our DNA changes in "response" to its environment. When Bruce first published his research, he was harshly criticized for his views. Now, in molecular biology, the idea that DNA is dynamic is no longer even debated and is accepted as a given. But at the time, this was considered a major paradigm shift. Before this, the accepted theory was DNA to RNA to protein, with one way arrows denoting this dogma. We now know that's not the case at all. In fact, the chart is still called the dogma of molecular biology but it's more complex. Instead of a unidirectional flow, the arrows are going back and forth, this way and that. Our knowledge of genetics has changed from a simple linear pathway to a much more complex interaction, including the role of environment and perception. This is a huge breakthrough.

These findings, that your environment directly affects gene expression at the DNA level, has enormous implications. First of all, a big part of your environment is your perception of that environment. If you perceive your environment to be a certain way, whether it actually is that way or not, your genetic expressions will be affected accordingly. You are 100 percent in control of your perception of your environment. Even if you have a genetic problem, it doesn't mean there is nothing you can do.

Epigenetics suggests that there are mechanisms to compensate for a genetic problem or predisposition. Of course, we do have to be realistic. There may be certain biochemical and physical limitations but you can always improve your condition through the focus of your intentions. This is my goal in *"**Intention Heals**"* – to show how the latest biological research supports our ability to influence our own health – and, with the workbook, to provide a step-by-step guide for achieving this.

Back in the laboratory, I have done some EEG studies where I influenced brainwaves of individuals through my intentions. Statistically significant results have been observed. Similarly, in another study I was able to influence a normally unvarying laser beam to change (to a statistically significant degree) through my intentions. Our intentions do affect our physical reality.

Know what needs to change for your particular imbalance to be corrected efficiently. Know that metabolic processes are dynamic, allowing change to occur; then use your intentions to manifest this difference.

Cultural Paradigms and Human Nature

"If you find a path with no obstacles, it probably doesn't go anywhere." - Unknown

For some readers, this material may be familiar and not particularly startling. For others, you may be feeling quite skeptical. I can understand a skeptic's reaction considering the history of new scientific discoveries and how human nature typically responds.

Consider the history of paradigms and human nature. It's amazing to look at the different concepts over the years that were once considered absolutely ridiculous and now they are considered just common sense. I very strongly believe that using intention to facilitate healing will one day become one of these concepts considered to be common sense. Using the least invasive healing modalities first is logical but this is not usually practiced in our society. Encouraging people to use their minds to influence changes in their bodies is considered a complementary therapy.

At present mainstream medicine uses toxic substances to induce cascades of unknown interactions in our bodies. There will come a day when we will be shocked that this was the first choice of treatment, similar to how we now feel about bleeding the patient which was a commonly accepted medical protocol in the 18th century. In the future we will look back at what we're doing now in amazement, as we are overlooking the incredible power of intentions in healing. There is now so much solid evidence for healing with intention that the data would fill volumes. In short, I feel that harnessing self-empowerment through focused intention is the way of the future in medicine.

One story that demonstrates how hard it is to shift the paradigm of mainstream thought is that of Dr. Ignaz Semmelweis, a once highly-respected physician. In 1847 he proposed that washing hands and cleaning operating room instruments before procedures would reduce the mortality rate. He was met with harsh criticism from the medical community and ultimately lost his medical practice. People listened to the medical authorities and no one wanted anything further to do with him and his ridiculous idea.

Now we think that this is just common sense but other physicians at that time cited many reasons to discredit Dr. Semmelweis. First, his claim lacked any scientific basis because no theory existed to explain the transfer of disease (germs) between patients by dirty hands or tools. You have to remember this was before Louis Pasteur's work in the1860's, so there was no scientific evidence to explain how something invisible could transfer between two individuals. This is analogous to the situation of healing with intention. We know it's happening but we don't have a mechanism to prove how it can happen, especially over great distances. I see many similarities between the resistance to the belief in hand-washing and resistance to the belief in healing with intention.

As a result of the unfortunate experience of Dr.. Semmelweis, someone has coined the phrase "the Semmelweis reflex." This amazing phenomenon describes a not uncommon human reaction - automatically dismissing or rejecting out of hand new information without thought, inspection or experiment. It is interesting that this reaction is still very common, even 140 years later. Some people are unable to even consider healing by intention, energy healing or healing at a distance and reject the concept immediately, even though they've literally done zero reading on the subject. They have had no experience in the field of energy healing or healing with intention, yet they dismiss it from a stance of total ignorance. That is the Semmelweis reflex.

Where are you on the Semmelweis reflex spectrum? You may have little or no skepticism since you are reading this book but you probably have encountered individuals who have quite rigid Semmelweis reflexes. First they say "there is no data" and when shown data, either refuse to look at it or describe it as "flawed," a judgment reached ahead of time. People will only accept new ideas when they are ready to do so.

This attitude may be easier to tolerate in others if we recognize that the resistance to change is a universal human trait, found even at times in those of us who consider ourselves open-minded. I have great respect for scientists who are willing to hold true to their convictions in spite of resistance from mainstream thought.

> *"Whenever you find that you are on the side of the majority,*
> *it is time to pause and reflect." - Mark Twain*

Healing Influences

"Healing is a process that occurs throughout your entire life, rather than a static state of well-being." - Adam

Most people think that healing is complete when the symptoms of a particular ailment cease to bother them. This implies that health issues are completely isolated from one another with no interaction. However, we know this is not true, as healing in a holistic sense involves physical, mental, emotional and spiritual wellness. None of these systems functions separately, so successful healing encompasses your entire being. When all of these systems are in balance, illness can be avoided or controlled.

Your healing is affected by both external and internal influences. It is important to remind ourselves what these are, in order to become **proactive** rather than **reactive**.

External Influences

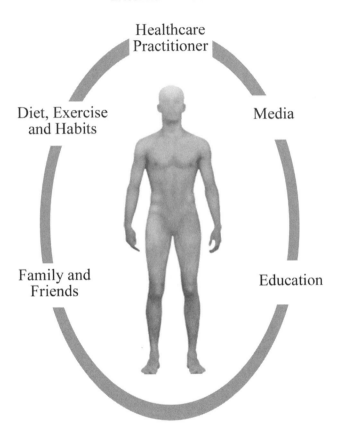

External Influences

Healthcare
Practitioner

Diet, Exercise
and Habits

Media

Family and
Friends

Education

What Influences You Externally?
Let's look carefully at how we form our perceptions.

Influence of Authority: Your beliefs are influenced by "expert information of the day" from the medical system, media, teachers, religious leaders and others you perceive as authorities. These are our cultural "authorities" or our cultural paradigm. Any time you receive a message, be mindfully aware of what you are being told and why.

Ask yourself:

What is the message I am receiving?
Who does this message serve?
Is what I am being told helpful to me?
Does this information conform to what I know intuitively?

Know that how you perceive events is how your **intentions affect your reality**.

I will focus my discussion of cultural paradigms on the following external influences:

1. Healthcare practitioners
2. The media
3. The educational system
4. Family and friends
5. Diet, exercise and habits

1. Your Healthcare Practitioner

"Make your own recovery the first priority in your life."
- Robin Norwood

Your healthcare practitioner plays a very dominant role in your health. Since medical authorities are often the source of expert medical opinion, they are the ones who deliver the results of your medical tests to you. How they convey this information is critical to your expectations and, consequently, your overall well-being.

We are highly suggestible to those we have placed in positions of authority. Their words, demeanor and actions have an enormous impact on our beliefs and, consequently, our ability to recover from illness.

Receiving a challenging diagnosis is a moment in your life when time seems to stand still and you hang onto every word from your healthcare professional. Remember to step back and observe your automatic reaction at such a moment. It is essential that the physician or practitioner frame predictions in as positive a manner as possible. Even with medically-accurate "incurable" diagnoses, nobody knows what the future holds.

For some patients, the diagnosis and discussion of their future is presented in a helpful and hopeful manner. However, I have heard many horror stories which send chills down my spine. One lady I helped with pancreatic cancer went to her doctor with her husband to get the results of her scan. The doctor said, "I have good news and I have bad news. The **good news** is that you do not have to plan for retirement. The ***bad news*** is the cancer is back and growing faster than ever. I advise you to get your affairs in order as you only have a few months to live. " It is hard to imagine a well-meaning physician being so disconnected from understanding the impact his words, thoughts and intentions have.

After this couple left that appointment, they started planning for her imminent death, as if this were a certainty. Fortunately it clicked with them that there is hope and there are alternative possibilities. In fact, it is currently more than five years later and this woman is now cancer free. There is no such thing as false hope, as nothing in healing is certain. It is important for healthcare practitioners to understand how powerfully their words and attitudes affect a patient's mind and, therefore, his or her healing process.

"He who has health has hope; and he who has hope has everything." - Arabic Proverb

Your medical professional may make the following statements or convey these opinions indirectly when they feel that there is very little they can do medically. Let's look at these common sayings more carefully.

A. It's in your genes: While DNA is clearly the blueprint of life for cellular reproduction, its information is dynamic, interactive and adaptable, as I described. Our DNA is not written in stone. The genetic material in every cell in your body is DNA which is very dynamic. (This is the new science.) Gene expression can be influenced through subtle energies. In other words, thoughts and feelings can influence and reprogram our physical selves.

B. It's all in your head: Sometimes when healthcare practitioners cannot find a physical cause for your symptoms, they resort to the idea that you are imagining your physical distress. This is not helpful. In fact, your symptoms are real and signal an imbalance in the body/mind/spirit entity that you are. I teach, however, that the source of righting this imbalance *is* "in your head," –that is, in the intentions of your mind. All of our symptoms are ultimately subject to change according to our beliefs. Unfortunately, this awareness is not behind the pejorative statement "It's all in your head."

Whether you are confident with your diagnosis or not, remember that your thoughts are translated by your brain; then your brain modifies your body to accommodate those thoughts via the release of biochemicals and activation of receptors. Ultimately you have control over that thought and hence the entire cascade of the biochemical reactions it triggers.

C. Nothing can be done: This statement again conveys the very real helplessness that a medical professional often feels. I am here to tell you that there is always something that can be done. Do your own research into other approaches to healing such as: energy healing, chiropractors, massage, naturopathic, acupuncture, Ayurvedic medicine, shamans, homeopathy, vitamin therapy, life style counseling and hypnotherapy. Combine any of these with your own intention to heal with your focused visualizations.

D. It is in your family history: The medical history of your family may be based on their particular lifestyle and environmental circumstances. This may have little bearing on your health as you have control over many of these issues which your parents and grandparents perhaps knew little about. It is important to make the necessary changes to improve your own lifestyle and environment.

E. It's only placebo: Ironically, this idea is used to discredit the very mechanism that works best: what you believe to be true is what works. This is the definition of the placebo effect. The placebo effect is often used as a dismissal rather than acknowledgement of this all-important mind-body connection. *Your body does not distinguish between a chemical process and your thought of that chemical process occurring.*

The body's ability to react to your beliefs often results in actual physical changes in your body. This occurs in any healing modality including Western medicine. That is the power of the mind and throughout this book you will learn to harness this force to your benefit. A first step is to notice any of your limiting beliefs that confine you to the old paradigm of separation between mind and body.

Many prescription drugs are actually impure placebos. (Spinney, L. (2006) "Purveyors of Mystery", *NewScientist.*) Psychiatrist Patrick Lemoine states that "the most reliable estimates suggest that around 35-40 percent of all official prescription drugs are impure placebos, by which I mean pharmacologically inactive substances contaminated with a tiny amount of active ingredient- not enough to have a clinical effect but enough for doctors to claim it does."

"Numerous studies have shown," Dr. Lemoine continues, "that while severe depression responds well to antidepressants, mild depression responds no better to these drugs than to placebo." Dr. Lemoine goes on to say, "Doctors continue to prescribe them because the act of prescription is such an integral part of the ritual of the medical consultation. They find it impossible to send a patient away empty-handed. The patient... expects to come away with a prescription."

Recent news of the ineffectiveness of anti-depressants hit the world's media. Many doctors are still convinced that their patients improve after taking them and they are probably right. One researcher says, "We're not saying that the drugs don't work. We are saying that the drugs might work for reasons other than they are thought to work. This is the power of the person's belief- that something they're doing is going to be effective- is a huge and misunderstood thing that could help people incredibly and save a lot of money if we could harness it better." (Canwest News, (2008)-*National Post.*)

Our intentions and expectations are extremely important in any healing modality. If placebo has significant results, imagine healing with your intentions trained to be focused on your health challenge! That is what ***Intention Heals*** is all about. It is understood that we all possess this mind-body control. NOW you will learn how you can harness and maximize this power by using your own intentions and expectations.

2. The Media

"In the spider-web of facts, many a truth is strangled."
- Paul Eldridge

Nearly everyone watches TV, reads the newspaper, uses the internet or listens to the radio. These all play a major role in shaping our beliefs and expectations. I used to think that if a journalist had only positive film footage about a story that the show would reflect this. For instance, a large US network filmed one of my workshops and interviewed attendees. They asked me ahead of time to find people who no longer had their illnesses. Many brought their medical records from their first diagnosis to their most recent tests, showing that their health issues had been resolved and were willing to discuss their healing experience on camera.

We naively thought that the media would be excited to report these amazing stories from people who had medical proof of their improvements. They interviewed all of them and reported none. After several similar experiences I became acutely aware that the world of media creates what it wants to report. If all of the information they filmed is positive but the mandate of the broadcast is controversy, then that is what they will produce. When they have control of the edit button that is pretty easy to do. The over-dubbed narration will also be manipulated to that end.

The media creates according to its needs. The major advertisers dictate what we see because the media must keep them happy in order to survive. What is portrayed is what someone else wants us to see, hear and think. We must be able to separate the editor's opinion from the real facts of the story, as often the media lags behind the progressive attitudes of many listeners.

How wonderful it would be if the focus was most frequently on something good that has happened rather than a sensational negative story. There are so many positive stories that could be covered and we could all learn something that would help us grow, both individually and as a global community. Many positive stories as well as alternative ways of looking at world events are now available on the internet. Let's do what we can to promote this positive change of focus.

3. The Educational System

"I have never let my schooling interfere with my education."
- Mark Twain

Our educational system influences how we think and react to events in life, including illness. Wouldn't it be inspiring if we were taught at an early age how to access the amazing powers within ourselves? Self-empowerment through our intentions should be integrated into our educational system, giving us lifelong confidence in the skills for creating our own reality. What a progressive and important addition to the school system this would be! For example, children could be taught to use their intentions to assist with healing minor sports injuries as well as help with all aspects of their school-age lives. Intentions can also be used to help with their grades at school.

Although it is still a rarity, there are now some integrative and holistic educational programs available. There is a movement afoot to combine basic educational knowledge with spiritual/holistic awareness. Eventually all children will have the opportunity to reach their highest possible potential as multi-dimensional thinkers.

"There is only one sound method of moral education.
It is teaching people to think." – Everett Dean Martin

4. Influence of Family and Friends

"Friends are the Angels that help you fly"
-Julia VeRost

Everyone has relatives or friends whose outlook is usually positive and others who are more often negative. Your mind is subconsciously picking up all of these signals, interpreting them and acting on them in your body. Keep in mind that the energy from positive individuals is translated by your body as positive intentions and will assist in your healing process.

5. Diet, Exercise and Habits

"We are what we repeatedly do. Excellence then,
is not an act but a habit." - Aristotle

You have control over what goes into your body, physically, emotionally and spiritually. Diet is the most physical aspect of what you are "feeding" yourself, so treat yourself with the respect that you deserve. Eating wisely is an obvious step in your healing. Make sure that you are drinking lots of water as this will clean your body by stimulating all body processes. Later in this workbook, I suggest that you write down what you physically "feed" yourself and view this list objectively. You would encourage someone you love to eat properly, exercise and quit harmful habits. Love yourself enough to do the same for yourself.

As you review your diet, exercise and lifestyle habits, consider what you ***actually do*** versus ***what you can do***. Consider what steps you can take to narrow this gap. We are all creatures of habit. Choose positive habits and integrate changes into your everyday lifestyle. Following this workbook will help you to begin making changes today.

Internal Influences

"I am the master of my fate; I am the captain of my soul."
- Ernest Henley

Internal influences consist of two parts:
A: the cues from within your body
B: how your mind interprets those cues.

Your interpretation of these cues contributes to your unique world view which has also been shaped by external influences. As you think carefully about your internal messages in the following discussion, you can synchronize your healing intentions precisely with these signals.

You can also change your interpretation of internal cues – that is, change your beliefs which I will talk more about. For most of us, being willing to change our interpretations is the key, because nearly all of us have limited views about what our senses tell us and what is actually possible. Healing using your intentions requires that you know your intentions are synchronized, or aligned with your beliefs.

Let's look at how we can understand these internal influences and change our minds to incorporate greater possibilities.

Internal Influences

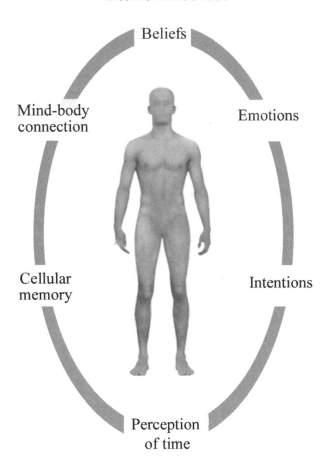

Beliefs

Mind-body
connection

Emotions

Cellular
memory

Intentions

Perception
of time

1. Beliefs (The mental integration of all influences)

"The difference between a flower and a weed
is a judgement." - Anonymous

Beliefs are the mental constructs which are the integration of all influences. Our beliefs act as a filter for all incoming information. Many times I have been asked about how someone's religious beliefs affect their healing. Intentional healing is inclusive of everyone and all belief systems. Whatever your religious beliefs are, this is likely a powerful influence on you. Use your beliefs in your visualizations to increase the impact they have on your well-being. Beliefs are a very powerful form of intention.

I've discussed the external cultural factors which influence belief, yet remember that you have an edit button at your control. You experience what you decide to, as you learn to "*take control*" of the experience, rather than feel victimized by it.

Change is the operative word. You are able to change your experience once you understand how powerful your mind is and how elastic your beliefs are. Be proactive by choosing how you want to feel rather than simply reacting out of habit. This will be only a theory until you decide to try it and find out for yourself.

"She didn't know it couldn't be done, so she went ahead and did it."
- Mary's Almanac

Recall the analogy about the elephant tied to a post. If you tether an elephant to a small post with a rope that is simply placed over the top of the post, the elephant is unable to move away because he believes he is tied up. Obviously, with his massive strength, all the elephant has to do is walk away. He is only tied up by his belief. And so are we.

Remember the last time you lie down on the green grass and gazed up at the sky. Staring up at this dynamic canvas of nature tempts our imagination. Every passing cloud, forming and evaporating into oblivion, stirs an awareness of something, someone or someplace in our memory. Fleeting images of shapes billow and disappear as we reflect on their likeness within our reality. Just when we are satisfied that we have the portrait nailed, it morphs into something else. It is easy to get totally immersed in the impressions we imprint from our imagination onto our own personal work of nature's art. There are no limits to what we can imagine.

"Imagination is more important than knowledge."
- Albert Einstein

Likewise there are no limits on how we can interpret what we hear, smell, taste and touch. If we focus on the moment as we lie there, we are instantly aware of the sound of running water from the stream not far away, birds chirping in the trees and the sound of the leaves blowing in the breeze. We can breathe in deeply and appreciate the light scent of the blossoms on the trees and bushes surrounding the field; taste the sweetness from the purple clover flower that we are chewing on, as we enjoy this sensual experience. We can feel the prickly softness of the grass we are lying on. We can even appreciate the occasional buzzing of an insect mindfully focused on its duties. Perhaps an ant crawls up our sleeve but we just ignore it in our state of blissfulness.

What an awesome movie you have created! One that is so much more than what has physically occurred. Most people describe their experiences only by using the five senses within four dimensions of space/time. These are just the immediate sensory facts, one tiny piece of the unlimited experiences open to us.

Some theoretical physicists currently estimate that our physical reality consists of 11 dimensions. (Polchinski, J.(1998). "String Theory", Cambridge University; Vol. 998.) How many of these dimensions might it be possible to access? New discoveries using particle accelerators to study dark matter and gravity are constantly expanding this number of dimensions as we continue the struggle to make sense of the material world within our scientific paradigms.

Ultimately no matter what scientific discoveries are made, you determine the creation of your own reality and how you respond to it. So back to the movie you are creating as you lie on the grass. Your subjective experience is linked to how your awareness interacts with all that you think and feel, including your perception of the passage of time. You determine how you respond to your environment.

You are constantly creating and recreating what you are experiencing. You are the movie producer, editing what you have experienced, are experiencing and will experience. Become proactive and understand that you have control over every aspect in your life's movie.

2. Emotions

"Human behavior flows from three main sources:
desire, emotion and knowledge" - Plato

Emotions are the feelings associated with intentions. You determine how you feel about your life's movie. Your emotions are a choice – and you can make a different choice; that is, you can change your beliefs about your emotions.

Sometimes we want to blame something or someone outside of ourselves for how we feel. It is only natural when confronted with a serious illness to ask "Why me?" Rather than taking the victim's stance, ask yourself "How does this illness serve me? What does it do for me? Does it alter any of my relationships? Does it allow me to do something or behave differently than I would otherwise?" Ask yourself these questions and you are well on your way to begin the healing process. These questions will bring to your awareness the needs that you must address, changes you must make and any faulty thinking you must dismiss. Rather than feeling victimized, you have taken a first step toward self-empowerment.

Let's look at how emotions work in your body. The emotions associated with your beliefs trigger the release of biochemicals and hormones. By placing yourself in a "happy state," you are controlling the release of serotonin and endorphins into your cells. If you choose to put yourself into a stressful mode, you have ordered yourself to release cortisol and epinephrine biochemicals. In both instances, your perception is creating your biochemical reality.

To break this down, emotions fuel or propel your thoughts. An intention, thought or memory stimulates neurons analogous to the way electricity completes a circuit. An emotion triggers neurons to emit a particular frequency which then triggers the release of biochemical correlates for a specific emotion. In many cases of physical illness, emotions play a major role. Your thought patterns guide which emotions you feel most intensely which, in turn, release biochemicals. You can decide how you want to react to a situation.

With a serious illness it is difficult to escape the feeling of fear as you face an uncertain future. Notice the fear, remember the power of your mind and decide to let go of the fear. Your point of power is not the future but the NOW. Practice releasing fear. Change your mind about feeling helpless. Remember - that's just a habit that you can change. *Trust the Process* of your own healing abilities.

Just as emotions can intensify your health problem if left uncontrolled, you can also use them to your betterment. Rather than repressing your emotions, the workbook section in this book guides you through retraining your reactions and responses. You can rationally decide how you are going to react to a situation through practice and exercising control.

3. Intentions

*"Power is the capacity to translate
intention into reality and then sustain it." - Warren Bennis*

Intentions are goal-based thinking. What happens in your body with an intention? An intention activates neurons in your brain by actually sending signals from one neuron to another, alerting your entire being.

On the larger scale, when you think a thought, your neurons send signals far beyond your physical body as they resonate at your own unique frequency. Your resonance connects you to the universal energy field which can be described as the collection of all information about everything in the universe and its connection to everything else. This field is present in all places and at all times simultaneously linking all past, present and all probable future events. It is a template for information exchange; a template we can actually access with focused intention. We are truly awesome beings.

Your body consists of trillions of cells and there are countless chemical reactions taking place every second. All these reactions are influenced on the molecular level by your intentions which is the driving force that manipulates energy and information systems.

Healing Influences

When you expect a positive outcome, you send that intention within yourself, initiating a cascade of biochemical reactions in your body. Your intention has set everything into motion to influence events so they are aligned with your thoughts. Your intentions affect things far beyond your conscious awareness. Your body does listen to what you are telling yourself and reacts accordingly. Talk about taking control!

You are responsible for the well-being of every cell in your body, just as a parent is responsible for its off-spring. Think in terms of parenting your cells, as you provide only what is best for them. Feed your cells the best possible ingredients for optimal physical and mental health. Encourage yourself with positive thoughts, just as you would inspire your child.

As I explained in the science tutorial, there is a growing body of proof that our thoughts and intentions influence our biological pathways which in turn influence the healing process. It has been proven experimentally that mental images and intentions directed to specific parts of our body do in fact produce significant physiological changes.(ADER,R.(1981).*Psychoneuroimmunology.*)Specific intentions appear to alter the frequency of energy fields which give direction to specific healing pathways.

One such experiment was conducted by HeartMath Research Center on the effect of conscious intention on human DNA. (R. McCraty, G.Rein, et al.(2003). "Modulation of DNA Conformation by Heart-Focused Intention", HeartMath Research.) Experiments show that DNA actually altered its shape when researchers intentionally focused different emotions toward the DNA.

When researchers sent loving emotions toward the DNA samples, the DNA strands lengthened or unwound as if in a relaxing mode. Conversely, when researchers sent anger, fear or stress toward the DNA, it tightened up and became shorter. Coiling directly relates to gene expression. This opens up the amazing possibility that our minds may be able to consciously change the DNA expression.

Quite literally, the shape of your future is ultimately your decision. You create the shape of things to come. You will manifest that which you focus on.

"Change is a choice." - Adam

You can make a conscious effort to change your automatic stress reactions. You can learn to react to situations with a more loving response. Make a habit of putting yourself in the other person's shoes. For instance, the next time a telemarketer calls you, resist the temptation to react with abruptness or anger.

Stop for a moment. Instead, imagine that the person at the other end of the phone is working hard every day in a third world country to feed his family. Imagine all the hours he or she has taken to learn another language so that they can do their job. Then respond with a more understanding and compassionate reaction. By doing this repeatedly in all kinds of situations, you can reprogram yourself for change.

4. Perception of Time

"Time is what prevents everything from happening at once."
- John Archibald Wheeler

What you sense is based on what you can imagine sensing. Remember, the mind is unlimited. How we each interpret events is unique. Courtrooms depend on this phenomenon. Eye witness accounts differ, not because the witnesses are lying but because they have different filters and see and experience the same event differently. Your perception of time is one of those filters.

Think of NOW as a bridge. On one side of the bridge is our past, comprised of all events, probabilities and choices that have led us to our NOW. On the other side of the bridge is our future containing all the possible and probable realities. The bridge, or our NOW, is our point of control and power through our intentions.

Imagine that you want to influence a future point in time; perhaps you have an exam the next day. You have studied diligently but still feel anxious. Visualize your future self sitting down calmly to write the exam. Visualize opening the exam paper and all the questions looking familiar to you. The questions deal with just the information that you have prepared for. See yourself writing down all the answers knowing that they are correct. The more realistic you can make this visualization, the more prepared you will be for this future event.

This is how we can change "future" events through our intentions. In changing your future you are also changing your perception of past events. For instance if in the past you felt fear when writing an exam and you stayed with that intent, this would have an effect on how well you do on the exam. However you have decided in the NOW that you are going to change your future by visualizing, as I mentioned previously. Thus you are simultaneously changing your perception of the past.

Breathing in the elemental gas ARGON is an interesting example of a thought in time. As it is a non-reactive gas, argon exists in our atmosphere now in the same form that it has for billions of years. Imagine all of the changes that Earth has experienced since the beginning of our planet's existence. Now take a deep breath... This breath of fresh air includes some of the atoms that were also breathed in by the first humans to walk upright. Doesn't this blur the rigid lines we draw between past, present and future?

Our physical and mental perspective of the passage of time is an individual experience. In the movie "Little Rascals," a five-year-old referred to an event that had happened five years previously as the beginning of time. From his perspective, it was the beginning of time. Likewise we all have our own concept of the passage of time in relation to how it impacts our lives. Time is only structured through the eyes of the beholder: YOU.

"The whole life of man is but a point of time; let us enjoy it."
- Plutarch

5. Cellular Memory

"Memory is the diary that we all carry about with us."
- Oscar Wilde

Cellular memory is the theory that memories, including habits and interests, are stored in every cell of the human body. Each cell in your body is a unique distinct living entity while, at the same time, all of your cells are functioning together uniformly as one living organism. Every cell has the ability to carry out the functions of any organ in the body. Every cell has its own immune and digestive functions and skeletal structures. Every cell also stores memory and emotion.

In order for such a unified multi-cellular organism to function, there must be an effective communication mechanism between all of the cells. The nervous system accounts for much of this communication but there is more than just nerve cells that links every cell together. Biochemical pathways provide an inter-cellular link, yet this does not fully explain the synchronicity between distant cells. Another communication mechanism must exist.

I describe this undiscovered communication mechanism as "what is looking through your eyes". It is activated by the frequency of your unique energy that coordinates every cell in your body to truly function as one harmonious unit: YOU!

Dr. Candace Pert, author of ***The Molecules of Emotion(1997)***, suggests that cellular receptors serve as connections between your memories, organs and mind. The energy of emotion is dynamically stored in all living organisms. This dynamic process is referred to as cellular memory.

There are many interesting reports of organ transplant recipients who have exhibited changes which reflect traits of the donor (G.Schwartz, L.Russek, P.Pearsall, (2002)"Changes in Heart Transplant Recipients That Parallel the Personalities of Their Donors." *Journal of Near-Death Studies.)* One of these cases follows a 47-year-old male who received a heart from a 17-year-old male. After the transplant the recipient was surprised by his new-found love of classical music. What he discovered later was that the donor loved classical music and played the violin. The 17 year-old had died in a car accident with his violin in hand.

Cellular memory is an important physiological part of our mind-body connection. An example of a childhood memory of mine illustrates this point. As a two-year-old, I was always reaching up to touch things on counter tops. My dad would always say the toaster is hot, the kettle is hot or the stove is hot. The meaning of the word hot meant nothing to me until one day I managed to touch the toaster when it was hot. Immediately the word hot became meaningful.

Experiencing "hot" made a connection in my mind through my nervous system and to my burned hand. My Dad reminds me that, instead of crying, I stared at my hand and repeated the word "hot". Now a meaningful connection in my memory had been formed. At that point, every cell in my body had experienced hot and the memory of this event was permanently imprinted into all of my cells.

We have all had similar experiences which have become hard wired into our cellular memory. Recalling some physical and/or emotional events sets off very strong memories. Focus your intention on changing not only the memories in your mind but the memories in your cells. In the Workbook exercises, you will be encouraged to use memory and emotion to your advantage by rewriting what occurred. You will learn to alter it according to your needs.

This book will guide you through your healing process by combining your conscious creativity with the more subconscious aspects of memory. As you progress through the Workbook, you will begin to experience a re-awakening to a higher state of awareness.

6. Mind-Body Connection

> *"What the mind dwells upon, the body acts upon."*
> *- Dennis Waitley*

The mind–body connection is precisely what I have been describing. It is our most direct and powerful access to our own healing potential. By strengthening both the mind and the body you maximize the potential of this vital bond.

To strengthen the body, every cell has to efficiently take in nutrients including oxygen. Breathing techniques and physical exercise stimulate this process, sending messages to your mind that you are serious about optimizing your physical conditioning. These small changes send signals to every cell in your body that you are willing to make changes. This is a pivotal point in strengthening your mind-body connection regarding your healing intention.

"What isn't tried won't work." - Claude McDonald

To strengthen the mind, consider the following; your brain, the physical mechanism of the mind, is the most complicated and profound computer ever created. It is estimated that you have 100 billion nerve cells in your brain (Huang,G. (2008) "Essence of Thought," *NewScientist;* Vol 198.) This gives your brain a processing capacity of 100 trillion, compared to 25 billion of an average desktop computer. That makes your processing capacity 4,000 times greater. Our brains also have the capacity to create 1 million new neuron connections per second, with an adult brain having 500 trillion synaptic connections.

What is most amazing about your brain is its adaptability and flexibility. It conforms to your own thought processes through expectations and is always rebuilding, repairing, rewiring and thereby recreating itself. A thought is translated in your brain; then your brain programs modifications to your body to accommodate that thought. What you think is what you get.

To optimize your well-being, reprogram yourself to maximize the functioning of your immune system. You must understand that before this can happen, you have to **want to change**. This may seem like an odd comment, as of course you want to change; you want to get better. In saying you want to get better, you must realize that change requires your focus on what influences you both externally and internally.

Your health is much more than just your physical well-being. Change requires that you address everything that influences you and how you view your reality. Your intention to change is sincere if it encompasses all aspects of you and your life.

There is no time like the present to start this process of change. Now is better than later, so don't delay. Show yourself that you are serious about your commitment for change. Make change your first priority. Remember that you can't fool yourself, as you know yourself too well. But you *can change yourself*.

"Believe that you have it and you have it." - Latin Proverb

Summary

New research in molecular biology shows that intentions affect your health by directly affecting your metabolism.

So how can you use this knowledge to your advantage?

Awareness is your first step toward change. Understand how your environment influences you. Become proactive in how you interpret these external signals. Your healing is influenced by external and internal events, yet how you are influenced is up to you. Your perception of how events influence you is ultimately what affects you, rather than the events themselves. It is important to take in only information which is helpful to you in your healing.

Your sincere intention must be your singular focus. Become self-reflective and totally honest. Focus on how you think, understanding how each thought flows into another and how your thoughts interact with one another. Intention aligns your conscious awareness with your subconscious thoughts and beliefs, getting every cell working toward the same goal, or on the same page, so to speak. Your conscious intention must be synchronized, or aligned with your subconscious intention.

Ask yourself, "What do I want?" Limit yourself to one desired outcome. If your answer is that you want to be healthy, say it aloud. Shout, "I want to be healthy!" Let it resonate within you that this is your intention. This is what you expect. Focus on the expectation that this will happen. Your perception of outcome makes a huge difference.

Change any habits or patterns that are not synchronized with your healing program. Absorb only information which is helpful to you. Let yourself know that you are seriously focused on the path toward change. This book will guide you along that path.

Follow the exercises in the workbook sections in the order that they appear, rather than skipping back and forth. It is designed sequentially with you in mind, making sure you are ready for each new step along the way. You will be comfortable with the material covered, pleased with your progress and ready to explore further.

Use the techniques contained in this guide book to give you that extra edge in healing.

Enjoy!

Workbook Section I

Building a Foundation for Visualizations

"We can use our conscious awareness to transform our lives by rewriting limiting perceptions, beliefs and self-sabotaging behaviors programmed in our subconscious minds."
- Dr. Bruce Lipton

Healing with intentions requires you to align your conscious intentions with your subconscious mind. Changing your perceptions of the past needs to be addressed before this can occur. Through following these exercises you will receive the maximum effect from this powerful process.

In order for you to get the best results, it is essential to do this section first. Dealing with these issues will prepare you mentally, physically and spiritually for the specific healing visualizations which follow. Although you may be eager to get into the visualizations themselves, don't shortchange yourself by cutting corners with this process. Skipping this step is like building a house without a foundation: it isn't going to be structurally sound. Solidly build your future wellness by following the sequence of this book. Heal your past by constructing a new more positive and optimistic view of your future.

It is recommended that you recreate the tables and charts in a larger format in order for you to accurately record and track your healing progress. Keeping a journal is one more step to tell your body that you are serious about making changes.

The following diagram lays out necessary topics you should address.

Workbook Section I Topics

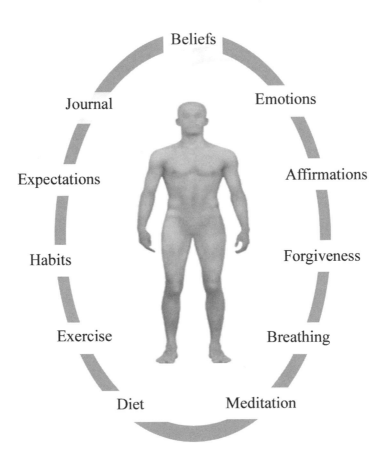

Beliefs

Journal

Emotions

Expectations

Affirmations

Habits

Forgiveness

Exercise

Breathing

Diet

Meditation

Change Limiting Beliefs

"When you change the way you look at things, the things you look at change." - Dr. Wayne Dyer

Our belief system is our own unique individual filter through which we view the world. Through experiences in life thus far, we have each formed our own way of processing incoming information in a way which we think is most useful to us. This interpretation of events may not be the most helpful to our development and growth if we are limiting our beliefs. Re-interpret past events to remove self-limiting beliefs.

Beliefs Reality Check

Let's explore some of your beliefs which could be limiting your effectiveness in healing through intentions. Be honest and open. Remember that you can't fool yourself. Note which of the following statements apply to you.

1: Limiting belief: I have no power to influence events. I react to events and do not create them. As such, I am a victim of circumstance.

Reality Check: Recent studies on the power of intention demonstrate that physical matter including DNA can be influenced through intention. Update the software in your mind according to these recent findings.

Alternate Positive View: I choose to use my power to influence my health.

How does limiting belief #1 relate to your situation and what can you do to change it?

_____

_____

"Doubt whom you will but never yourself." - Christine Bovee

**

2: Limiting belief: I don't deserve health and happiness.

Reality Check: **Health and happiness is not based on merit.** You CREATE your own health and happiness, so incorporate this reality into your thoughts, words and actions.

Alternate Positive View: I deserve health and happiness, because that is what I intend to CREATE.

How does limiting belief #2 relate to your situation and what can you do to change it?

_____

_____

"The only limit to our realization of tomorrow will be our doubts of today." - Franklin D. Roosevelt

**

3: Limiting belief: I fear death.

Reality Check: Everyone and everything alive will die eventually. It is a matter of when and under what circumstances. View death as a point of transformation rather than a finality. It is a new beginning. **Trust the process.**

Alternate Positive View: Death is a natural process and knowing this, I will live my life to the fullest.

How does limiting belief #3 relate to your situation and what can you do to change it?

_____

_____

"Nothing in life is to be feared. It is only to be understood."
- Marie Curie

**

4: Limiting belief: I always have bad luck.

Reality Check: You create your own reality and it is time you let yourself have better luck. Focus on the positive outcomes in your day. Don't sweat the small things!

Alternate Positive View: Many good things happen to me each and every day.

How does limiting belief #4 relate to your situation and what can you do to change it?

_____

_____

"Each misfortune you encounter will carry in it the seed of tomorrow's good luck." - Og Mandino

**

5: Limiting belief: Today will be worse than yesterday.

Reality Check: Intentions and thoughts are natural forces of nature just like gravity is. Think positively and you will attract positive events and expectations into your reality.

Alternate Positive View: I choose to have a happy day.

How does limiting belief #5 relate to your situation and what can you do to change it?

_____

_____

"Yesterday is gone. Tomorrow has not yet come. We have only today. Let us begin." - Mother Teresa

**

*6: **Limiting belief:*** I fear failing, therefore I won't take any risks.

Reality Check: Trust the process and believe in your success. Only what is attempted can be realized.

Alternate Positive View: I look forward to trying something new today.

How does limiting belief #6 relate to your situation and what can you do to change it?

_____

_____

"Just remember, 100% of the shots you don't take, don't go in."
Wayne Gretzky

**

*7: **Limiting belief:*** I have too much stress in my life.

Reality Check: Stress is the reaction that you have allowed yourself to experience. When an event triggers this reaction within you, ask yourself why you have chosen this response.

Alternate Positive View: I handle anything that comes my way in a calm stress–free manner.

How does limiting belief #7 relate to your situation and what can you do to change it?

_____

_____

"When it rains, I let it." - 113 year old man in response to a question about the secret of his longevity

These are a few beliefs which may be holding you back from your healing. List your own limiting beliefs and use the layout below to analyze and modify them.

Limiting Beliefs Exercise Table

Your Limiting Belief	Reality Check	Alternate Positive View

Healing Emotions

"Your heart often knows things before your mind does."
- Polly Adler

Emotions are feelings associated with thoughts and memories. The impact of negative emotions tends to settle like a log jam in a stream and block your energy flow. The issues around which this energy block occurs and the size of the blockage, differs in each of us. We all have our own unique blockages. Identify the feeling that shows up for you when you accumulate stress or the emotion that you express as a physical symptom. For example, what is your first physical reaction to a crisis? Do you get an instant headache, backache, stomach ache or the proverbial pain in the neck?

In your mind's eye, see the log jam of your emotional reactions and set your intention to BURST the dam in order for the natural healing stream to flow.

The following exercises will help you identify the impact on your daily life of all of the habitual emotional reactions you carry with you from your past.

Write your answers to the following questions as honestly and thoroughly as you can. Make sure that you have made an effort to dig deeply so that you leave no emotional stone unturned.

Emotional Challenge Exercise

1. What unresolved issue do you often revisit with anger? Does any of your anger involve blaming others?

_____

_____

_____

2. Do you feel guilt about any of your behaviors or decisions from the past?

_____

_____

_____

3. How has your guilt or anger affected your health?

_____

_____

_____

4. How has your health affected your emotional state?

_____

_____

_____

5. If you could go back in time, what major stress situations would you deal with differently?

_____

_____

_____

Steps to Positively Influence Your Emotions

1. Review what you have written in this exercise. Note that some of your emotions are based on repetitions of fragmented ideas with no apparent solutions. Some issues tend to replay over and over.
2. Underline any of your answers that are repetitions.
3. Close your eyes and reflect on the issues and recurrent themes you have noted. In self-talk, what ideas do you reinforce? Question yourself as to why you habitually have that particular thought. For instance, in reflecting on your use of the phrase, "I always have trouble in relationships," you may not be sure whether this thought was a result of past events or whether your experience was influenced by your negative thought in the first place.
4. Identifying these self-limiting reactions is the first step. Now you must actively work on modifying or eliminating them.
5. Identify what triggers habitual negative emotions in you. What or who reinforces your negative thoughts and emotions about events? How can you change them? Write your healthier responses below:

Modified Emotional Responses

1. How will you, more positively, deal with your unresolved issue of anger?

_____

_____

_____

_____

2. How will you, more positively, deal with your feelings and thoughts which may have allowed your condition or illness to develop?

_____

_____

_____

_____

3. How will you, more positively, deal with your feelings of guilt or blame about any issues that might have contributed to your illness?

_____

_____

_____

_____

_____

4. How will you, more positively, deal with the relationship between your health condition and your emotional state?

_____

_____

_____

_____

Practice Empowering Affirmations

"First say to yourself what you would be; and then do what you have to do." - Epictetus

Affirmations are short declarations of truth which you should say aloud to yourself in order to reinforce your intention. Reflect on how your habitual negative self-talk can be reframed. For example, the phrase "I **always** have trouble in relationships" leaves no room for alternatives. Reword it in a positive framework such as "*I am forming positive relationships with others.*"

General Affirmation Exercise

It is important to set aside a regular time in your day to do affirmations. Many people prefer to do them in the morning, as they reinforce how your day will be. As you face a mirror, be sure to look into your eyes as you address yourself in order to emphasize your sincerity. Believe in yourself and what you are telling yourself.

Express your gratitude and appreciation as you improve an aspect of your life by doing these exercises.

Focus on these words as you express them aloud with feeling:
1. I love myself.
2. I love others and others love me.
3. I am happy with who I am and what I think, say and do.
4. I feel wonderful and am full of healing energy.
5. Today is a marvelous day full of new opportunities.
6. I am grateful for all the wonderful things that are in my life.

Those of you saying, "Yeah, sure but I don't really love myself," do this exercise anyway. Intend to begin loving yourself. Practice self-forgiveness and monitor your behavior as you begin to change.

Customized Affirmation Exercise

1. Review your answers to Modified Emotional response in the previous chapter on "Emotions".
2. Create your own affirmations from your specific emotional challenges.
3. Set aside a specific time in your day for doing affirmations.
4. Use your own statements to create your own customized affirmations.
5. Look into a mirror and make eye contact with yourself.
6. Focus on the words as you express them aloud with feeling and passion.

Modified Emotional Response Question (refer to the previous topic "Emotions".)	Response to Question	Affirmation
Example: How will you, more positively, deal with your unresolved issue of anger?	Example: I feel that my difficult divorce is the source of my anger issue. I will focus on the positive events upcoming in my own life, for instance my child's graduation.	Example: I have incredible inner strength and power within myself.
How will you, more positively, deal with your unresolved issue of anger?		
How will you, more positively, deal with your feelings and emotions which may have allowed your condition or illness to develop?		
How will you, more positively, deal with your feelings of guilt or blame about any issues that might have contributed to your illness?		

How will you, more positively, deal with the relationship between your health condition and your emotional state?		
How will you, more positively, deal with your feelings about stressful events in your past?		

Create Your Own Customized Affirmation Table:

These are your own unique issues. Remember YOU know YOURSELF better than anyone else.

Your Own Emotional Question	Response to Question	Affirmation

Heal Through Forgiveness

"To forgive is to set a prisoner free and discover that the prisoner was you." - Lewis Smedes

Forgiveness is an essential part of cleansing negative emotions. In the process of forgiving others, you must also forgive yourself. As the forgiver, empower yourself to let go of the past. Forgiveness allows you to live freely in the present moment.

Removing offending persons from your mind, or repressing your anger toward them, does not effectively free you from the issue. I knew someone who cut out the face in photographs of anyone she didn't care to see. It made an interesting collage of family photographs! In actual fact, what it did was EMPHASIZE who was missing, rather than eliminate them. They became more obvious in their omission.

Who are the key figures in your personal story? Think about people in your past who you feel have hurt you physically or emotionally. Ask yourself if you still hold ill feelings toward them.

"Forgiveness is the first step towards healing."
- Mark Twain

The following questions will help you look honestly at your personal story and how you got to where you are today.

1. Who are individuals that have made your growth and development more difficult?

_____

_____

_____

_____

2. What circumstances – by fate or choice – seem to have blocked your personal growth?

_____

_____

_____

3. Who are individuals or groups currently in your life who, if they behaved differently, would make your life easier?

_____

_____

_____

4. Has your story changed as you have changed over time? If so, how?

_____

_____

_____

5. How do you see your story changing from now on as you change your perspective?

_____

_____

_____

6. Go back and look at persons or events you listed as having an impact on you and try a different take on the situation. For example, do you understand better now what made a person behave as they did?

_____

_____

_____

7. Can you feel more compassion for how you responded at that time, given the person you were then?

_____

_____

8. Write down any altered versions you now have about your story and what you have always told yourself and others.

_____

_____

_____

The following table will bring to your awareness the specific people you need to forgive in order to move forward with your own healing. Fill in this chart with your most honest recollection of events and your responses and feelings about them. Project your feelings of love and forgiveness in your new response. Holding on to stress and anger blocks your energy flow.

Forgiving Others Table

Recall the Scene	Your Initial Response	Feelings About Your Response	Forgiveness Response
Example: Marital conflict which led to divorce.	*Example:* Anger, outrage and confusion.	*Example:* Wish I had reacted differently.	*Example:* I send him/her love and wish them the best in their future.

Forgiveness Visualization

Due to circumstances, it may be difficult to express your forgiveness in person. Remember that forgiveness can also be done non-locally at the level of the mind.

- *Imagine that you are having a conversation in a face-to-face meeting with the person you feel has wronged you.*
- *Visualize your conversation taking place in a casual and comfortable setting, allowing you to feel in your comfort zone as you convey your message of forgiveness.*
- *Make it as meaningful as possible, expressing how you felt when this happened and why.*
- *Explain how this has hurt you in your past and how you are forgiving them now, releasing this energy.*
- *In your mind and heart know it will be different now and in future.*
- *Visualizing this becomes easier to do with practice and you will feel lighter as you literally lighten your emotional load. Take a load off through the act of forgiveness.*
- *Create your own positive affirmation from this experience of forgiving.*
- *Consciously focus on learning to trust your wise, intuitive self.*
- *Allow yourself to love them and yourself.*
- *As you practice forgiveness, you will find over time that it becomes more sincere and heartfelt.*

Forgiving Yourself

Most of us are our own worst critics. Each and every one of us has a critical inner voice which influences our thoughts and behavior patterns. Many of us automatically hear this voice and, without any opposition, obey its call. It reinforces what we have thought previously by simply replaying it over and over again.

All of your good and bad experiences, all memories and their emotional impact, have been duly noted by your subconscious. Often the underlying repetitious themes are guilt and blame; the wrongs you have done to others and the wrongs others have inflicted on you. If this is the case, aren't your tired of carrying around this negative baggage?

In this section you will learn to listen to what you are automatically telling yourself. You can then decide to change your perception of yourself (your story) by seeing the lessons you have learned and how you have become more aware of your options to become a better person.

Here are three exercises to help you in your self-forgiveness work:

1. Forgiving Yourself Table
2. Visualization for Forgiving Yourself
3. Forgiving Yourself Exercise

In the table below, fill in the chart with your most honest recollection of events, your responses and feelings. Project feelings of love and forgiveness toward yourself as part of your new response.

Forgiving Yourself Table

Recall the Scene	Your Initial Response	Feelings About Your Response	Forgiveness Response
Example: I had an argument with someone I love.	Example: Anger.	Example: Wish I had been more rational and calm.	Example: I forgive myself for being angry and irrational. I am a calm and rational person seeking to find our commonalities rather than our differences.

2. Visualization for Forgiving Yourself

- *IMAGINE that you are having a conversation in a face- to-face meeting with the person you feel that you have wronged.*
- *Ask for their forgiveness.*
- *Explain how this has also hurt you in your past and how you are forgiving yourself now, releasing this energy.*
- *Create your own positive affirmation from this experience of forgiving yourself.*
- *Allow yourself to love yourself.*

3. Forgiving Yourself Exercise

- *Imagine a person that you admire and respect (for instance a friend or coworker)*
- *Explore your thoughts, images and feelings of admiration. Why do you admire and respect this person?*
- *Project those same feelings onto yourself. If they are normally patient with others, see yourself as being patient.*
- *Honor yourself in this process as you emulate these qualities.*
- *Practice this routine as you build respect and trust toward yourself.*

In summary, learn from past experiences and with that learning, recognize that the past is no longer relevant. Let it go.

Live freely in the present.

Practice Awareness of Breathing

"Breath is Spirit. The act of breathing is Living."
- Unknown

Breathing is essential to all your cells and your entire energy system. Through attention and intention, breathing in this vital life energy will become more efficient. All of us need to breathe air to survive, yet many people are unaware that they are taking shallow breaths and breathing just enough to function. It is important to breathe deeply during the exercises in this book in order to maximize their effects.

Diaphragmatic breathing is deep breathing. The diaphragm, located at the base of the lungs, is the major muscle used in breathing. Breathing from the diaphragm gets maximum oxygen to every cell which in turn reduces stress. That's why it's good to "take a deep breath" when you are upset. Practice the following diaphragmatic breathing techniques:

Diaphragmatic Breathing Techniques
(Can be used in conjunction with all visualizations)

1. Lie on your back on a flat surface such as a floor exercise mat or in bed. Support your head with a pillow and bend your knees with a pillow supporting them. If this is difficult for you, sit comfortably in an upright position.

2. Place one hand on your upper chest and the other on your

stomach, just below your ribs. When you breathe you can feel your diaphragm move.

3. Relax and inhale slowly through your nose, keeping your upper hand as still as you can.

4. Pause briefly: then by tightening your stomach muscles, exhale blowing air out from your mouth while keeping the hand on your chest still. In your mind's eye, release with your breath what you do not need or want in your body. In this way, rid your body of any emotional blockages and problems.

5. The timing for this breathing will vary between individuals. I recommend developing a pattern, or number sequence, so you can practice counting out these steps as you focus on your breathing. For instance, the pattern I use is what I call the **3-2-5** method.

    a) Take **3** seconds to breathe in (fill your lungs).

    b) Pause or hold your breath for **2** seconds.

    c) Release your breath over **5** seconds.

    d) Find a pattern, or number sequence, that is comfortable

      for you, as everyone has different lung capacities.

6. Repeat several times until you feel totally relaxed; up to 10 minutes.

Diaphragmatic breathing exercise:

Breathing While Lying Down

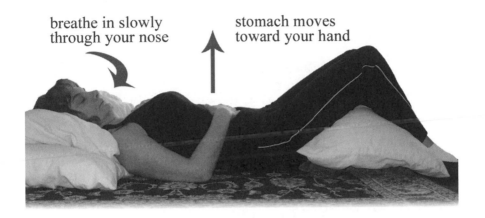

breathe in slowly
through your nose

stomach moves
toward your hand

Your goal is to supply more oxygen to your body.

> **SEE** yourself relaxed and breathing rhythmically.
>
> **FEEL** your breath flow slowly yet full of energy.
>
> **HEAR** the inhale and exhale of each breath in rhythm.
>
> **KNOW** that oxygen is reaching every cell in your body.
>
> **MAKE IT REAL**

Alternate diaphragmatic breathing exercise:

This same diaphragmatic breathing exercise can be done sitting on a chair in an upright position.

Breathing While Seated

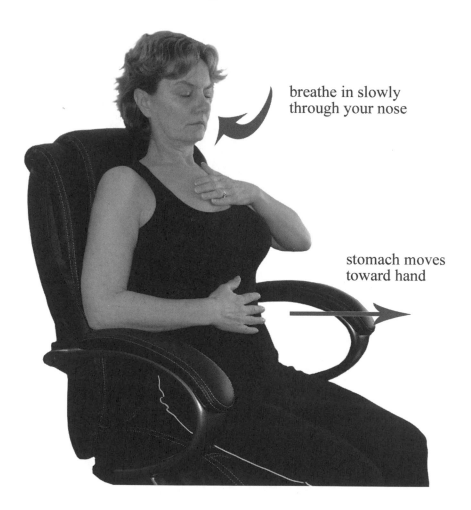

breathe in slowly through your nose

stomach moves toward hand

Through practice, this exercise becomes easy and effortless. Imagine when doing this that you are providing your body, mind and soul with everything you need to achieve your goal of wellness.

Practice Meditation

"When a man sits down in quietness to listen to the teachers of his spirit, many things will come to him in knowledge and understanding." - Chief Dan George

Meditation is quieting the mind, or stillness of mind. The goal is to shift attention from your conscious habitual thoughts to your subconscious so that you can listen to your wise inner self.

Habitual mind chatter drowns out your wise inner voice. Being still means letting go of your attention to this chatter. You can become a non-judgmental observer of your own thoughts, as if from a distance. Your intention to change to this focus, along with deep breathing, will relax you and help to bring about a state of heightened awareness.

This state of heightened awareness provides a link to your subconscious mind. Your intention to see "a new vision of self" is actually reprogramming your subconscious mind through enhancing your connection to the field of information during this state.

Preparation for Meditation

CONCENTRIC CIRCLES OF ENERGY EMANATE OUTWARD AND DOWN FROM THE CENTER OF YOUR BODY

EVERY MUSCLE IN YOUR BODY BECOMES RELAXED

1. Practice meditation daily. Some people prefer to meditate each morning while others prefer evening. See which time of the day resonates best with you.

2. Find a quiet place which is familiar to you; be in your comfort zone. Be sure that there are no ticking clocks, barking dogs or other distractions. As you become experienced with meditating you will be able to dismiss these distractions from your awareness.

3. Take 3 deep diaphragmatic breaths slowly in to your maximum input; then exhale slowly and completely. See and feel your entire body relaxing. (3-2-5 method).

4. From the top of your head imagine concentric circles of energy emanating a soft vibration or wave motion outward from the centre of your body, starting at the top of your head and going down toward your toes. Do this until every cell in your body is relaxed. Then imagine this energy moving up from your toes to your head and beyond.

5. In this relaxed state, your breathing has slowed.

6. How long you meditate is an individual decision. Experiment with it and do what resonates best or feels most comfortable.

7. Once you are in this meditative state, **know** that everything in your life is improving. Enjoy this feeling.

A Meditation Exercise

- *Release all thoughts from your awareness (shift your focus)*
- *In your state of meditation, HUM at a low, steady pitch.*
- *Feel yourself rising up and above your physical self.*
- *Focus on ascending up through the ceiling, roof, clouds, sky, stars and connecting to more energy as you ascend through a web of energy.*
- *At the same time as your ascension, raise the pitch of your hum gradually to higher and higher pitches and synchronize the tone with your ascension. There is always another octave higher even as it goes beyond the limits of audible sound.*
- *Imagine all of your cells vibrating to your HUM, as if you are a guitar string resonating at the same coherent frequency. Get every cell vibrating together in unison.*

During meditation, when in quietness of spirit, ask yourself a question. Ask for guidance on any topic or issue. You will receive guidance from all of the connections that you have within which includes your connection to this energy field of all information. This is called INTUITION.

Intuition is your personal, internal guidance system and your intentions are the controls. You are ultimately in control of your relationship with your past, present and future self, as well as your relationship with all others and the connections that you have and will make. Meditation will allow you to discover your intuitive self.

Diet Improvement

"When it comes to eating right and exercising, there is no "I'll start tomorrow."" - V.L. Allineare

A healthy diet is a great boost for healing your body and mind. Reduce junk foods to a minimum. Have fruits and vegetables around for ready snacks. Drink lots of water, preferably filtered. Pay attention to what foods make you feel good after you have eaten them. One key habit to longevity in diet issues is to stop eating before you feel full. Your intentions about improving nutrition register in your subconscious mind that you are serious about making changes.

Diet Question table

Diet Questions	Your Response	Your Affirmation
How could you improve your diet?	I can eat more vegetables and fruit.	I enjoy eating fruits and vegetables several times daily.
Do you tend to eat beyond what your body needs?	I find it hard to resist what is left on my plate even though I feel full.	I will put smaller portions on my plate.
Is there a category of foods that you consume but don't need?	I find it hard to resist sweets.	I enjoy a piece of fruit for dessert.
Do you find that you eat your dinner late in the evening?	I usually eat dinner late but I then find that food sits on my stomach while I sleep.	I enjoy eating early so I can sleep better.

Create your own questions as you see fit. Feel free to use any of the above responses and affirmations.

Your Diet Question table

Diet Questions	Your Response	Your Affirmation

Exercise Commitment

"Movement is a medicine for creating change in a person's physical, emotional and mental states." - Carol Welch

Exercise is essential to stimulate your immune system toward healing. It is wonderful if you are up to running a marathon but just a daily routine of a half hour brisk walk (or two 15-minute walks) will revitalize you both physically and mentally. Do what you are able to do. Note your current maximum range of activities and gradually expand this. If you are incapable of any movement, a visualization of exercise will help. You will be able to create a visualization of your exercise routine after you read the section on VISUALIZATIONS later in this book.

Example Exercise Question table

Exercise Related Questions	Your Response	Your Affirmation
Do you have a regular exercise program?	I don't have time for exercise.	I enjoy walking twice around the block and feeling invigorated.
Do you have a regular exercise program?	I am not well enough to waste my energy on exercise.	I enjoy doing my exercise routine and visualizing beyond this.
Do you focus on your breathing as you exercise?	I just don't think about it when I am exercising.	I feel reenergized when I am exercising and focusing on my breathing.

Your Exercise Question table

Exercise Related Questions	Your Response	Your Affirmation

Creating Helpful Habits

"Good habits result from resisting temptation."
- Ancient Proverb

Habits have physical, chemical and emotional components. Unhelpful habits can be broken and your mental software reprogrammed to your benefit. Begin by identifying the triggers, so that you can stop the behavior at its source. For instance, if stress triggers the desire for a cigarette, explore ways to interrupt your habitual chain of reactions. Of course, notice what you can do to decrease stress. Meanwhile, have something within reach other than cigarettes, such as carrot sticks or chewing gum.

The same may be said of any habit, such as drinking too much alcohol or overeating. Notice the triggers and substitute other ways to feel good. Excessive stress and poor lifestyle habits can be deeply ingrained. Nearly all unhelpful habits have emotional components as well as physical ones. Your goal is to achieve and maintain emotional balance by retraining your responses and establishing good habits.

Habit Question Table

Habit Related Questions	Your Response	Your Affirmation
Do you smoke?	Smoking relaxes me.	I enjoy breathing smoke free air.
Do your drink excessively?	I usually have a few drinks after work to unwind but it often turns into quite a few.	I enjoy time with my family when I am sober.
Are you critical of yourself?	I always put myself down when in conversations with others.	I enjoy the feeling of self confidence when I feel good about myself and express this to others.
Do you drink a lot of Pop (soda)?	It is inexpensive and readily available at many stores.	I enjoy drinking filtered water with a twist of lime as I find it refreshing.
Do you consume a lot of artificial sweeteners?	Artificial sweeteners are hard to avoid as they are in most drinks, baked goods, gums and candies.	I make a conscious effort to read the labels whenever I am purchasing products that may contain artificial sweeteners so that I can make an informed choice.
Do you feel that you overuse your cell phone?	It is so convenient and available.	I use land phones and text messaging as much as possible to avoid long conversations with the cell phone to my ear.

Create your own questions as you see fit. Feel free to use any of the above responses and affirmations.

Your Habit Question Table

Habit Related Questions	Your Response	Your Affirmation

Creating Your Intention Chart
(*Expectations*)

"Whatever we expect with confidence becomes our own self-fulfilling prophecy." - Brian Tracy

Expectations play a major role in creating your reality. In health issues, the expectation of getting better is a huge step toward recovery. When you expect a positive outcome, you send that healing intention within yourself and beyond yourself as you have set into motion everything needed to manifest that reality.

Project your future expectations by creating an **Intention Chart** which will help you activate your healing through intentions.

Write a list of what activities you have done in the past that you enjoyed, what you do for enjoyment now and what you want to do in the future. Find photos of these activities and start a collection of them. If they are photos of you, these images are imprinted in every cell as memory. Remember the sight, sound, smell, taste and feel of these activities. Become familiar with your recollection and emotional attachment to them. How do these photos move you? With confidence, project your past wellness and passion of activities you love into future events that you look forward to.

To create your ***INTENTION CHART:***

1. Find images of yourself or others doing activities that you once did or intend to do.

2. Paste your picture in the center of the chart with images of sports, hobbies and social activities pasted around your image. This chart is what you use to visualize your future activities or goals that you intend to reach. Some activities which you can use to create your INTENTION CHART are:

> Sports ...tennis, biking, swimming, hiking, running, etc.
> Hobbies… music, art, computers, gardening, cooking, etc.
> Social Activities… plays, movies, parties, dancing… etc.
> Work…career moves, academic pursuits .... etc.

3. Use your ***INTENTION CHART*** to focus on anything you want to achieve. For instance, if you are trying to find a job, find pictures of scenes to do with the type of job you would like and paste them around your image in the chart. Should you want to sell your house, make that your theme. If forming new relationships with people is your goal, create your chart accordingly.

In the following sample **INTENTION CHART**, health and physical activities are the primary focus.

Your ***Intention Chart*** gives you a clear visual representation of whatever you want to manifest into your reality. Focus on themes, thoughts, events or situations that you desire.

You have implanted this intention in your mind, and your body responds according to your instructions by initiating a cascade of biochemical reactions. You will attract all that is in accordance with your expectation, as you are influencing events and circumstances far beyond your conscious awareness. Intention is a powerful force which you can use to your advantage in every aspect of your life. Manifest your reality according to your intentions.

Imagine yourself within your ***Intention Chart*** as realistically as possible. Immerse yourself in every aspect of this reality; your new reality.

SEE yourself doing what you want to do in as much detail as possible.
FEEL how wonderful this experience is.
HEAR every detail in your awareness.
MAKE IT REAL.

Keep your Intention Chart in a place where you can focus on it often.
Look at it before bedtime and dream it into your reality.

Maintaining a Journal

"Goals are the fuel in the furnace of achievement."
- Brian Tracy

Many people find it helpful to keep a journal which documents their progress. Think of it as a daily diary specific to your healing. Maintaining a journal reinforces your goals by focusing on where you started and where you are headed. This is basically a road map of your healing journey.

Checklist

Use the checklist on the following page for the first week of your healing program. Make copies of this chart for continued use and keep them handy for your reference. The checklist is a tool for you to keep track of the various aspects of your healing program. Simply go through the list each day and check off the items you have worked on throughout the day. Eventually it will naturally become part of your daily routine.

Building a Foundation for Visualizations

Topic	Day1	Day2	Day3	Day4	Day5	Day 6	Day7
Beliefs							
Emotions							
Affirmations							
Forgiveness							
Breathing							
Meditation							
Diet							
Exercise							
Habits							
Intention Chart							
Journal Update							

Bedside Notes

"You must be the change you wish to see in the world."
- Mahatma Gandhi

Our subconscious thoughts are more accessible during our sleeping hours. Often we find answers in dreams or semi-awake states to questions that have bewildered us in our waking state. A good habit is to keep a note pad and pen on your bedside table. During the night, when you have an interesting thought revealed to you, jot it down. We dream to sort out new experiences and blend them with our reality.

Some mornings you may wake up surprised to see a blank piece of paper when you were sure you had written something down. You might have just dreamed that you wrote something, but this has jogged your memory. What you are aware of in your sleep may provide helpful clues and insights into the direction you need to take. Keep these notes handy for your own reference. Occasionally you will write something that makes perfect sense in your dream state but when reading it the next morning, it makes no sense. This is normal and be patient, as its meaning will eventually be revealed to you.

Summary of Workbook Section I

The exercises in ***Workbook Section I- Building a Foundation for Visualizations*** rewire your memory of events and your responses to them. Face your issues and unblock your energy flow. Consciously become aware of any ghosts from the past which you have brought into your present. Understand the triggers which have allowed these issues to affect you and modify how you perceive them. Then see yourself in a positive variation of the event- like the alternate ending to a movie on DVD. Revisit it frequently until it is realistic and comfortable as you integrate it into your life.

Change the pattern and change your past, present and future. Unlearn a negative pattern by replacing it with a positive one. Replace unhelpful memories using conscious thoughts until it becomes habit and your subconscious takes over this duty. These changes take time to become as habitual as the behavior you are replacing, so be patient. New neural pathways will be forged that will become helpful and more comfortable with practice through INTENTION. Show yourself that you can change.

Reward yourself for a job well done, like treating yourself to an activity you enjoy but seldom indulge in, such as going to the theater to watch a play, or to see a movie. Stimulating your pleasurable responses physically promotes your well-being because you will feel better. When you expect positive changes, your body releases a cascade of biochemicals, thus reinforcing your new reality. ***Now you KNOW that the power to change is within you!***

Workbook Section II

Introduction to Visualizations

"We are what we think. All that we are arises with our thoughts. With our thoughts we make the world." - Buddha

The question I am most frequently asked in my workshops is, "What visualization should I do for a specific ailment?" This Section of the Workbook contains visualizations for self-improvements and specific ailments. Find the one that is closest to your issue. In addition, you will learn how to add details to further customize your own visualizations. Over time you will find it necessary to modify them in order to maintain your focused attention and intention. In this section of the book, I lay out simple techniques and easy steps to customize your visualizations, tailor-made for you and by you.

To get started, ask yourself, "What changes in my health do I want?" Set your goals. Use your intention chart to get involved in the planning. *VISUALIZE* doing your daily routines in optimum health. Recreate yourself and explore your new reality.

The planning phase often seems to take forever before you get started. However, we've all experienced what happens if we skip these meticulous preparation steps. Just like travelling somewhere without planning in advance, it can ruin your entire vacation. Likewise, to achieve long-lasting benefits from using your **intentions to heal**, you must realize that laying the groundwork before this journey is just as essential as the journey itself.

To prepare your mind's eye for visualizations, you should sharpen your ability to think in pictures. Let's try a simple visualization that almost anyone can do. Close your eyes and mentally put yourself in your own living room. Be aware of all of your sensory input as you relax in your comfort zone. In your mind's eye see your computer, television set, see pictures on the wall and feel yourself comfortably sinking into your favorite chair. Hear the familiar sounds around your home such as the clock ticking inside and birds singing outside. Smell your delicious dinner baking in the oven. SEE, FEEL, HEAR, SMELL and TASTE this experience as you tune into all of your senses. Not too difficult to do, right?

Your goal is to become as comfortable and familiar using visualizations for your health as you are when visualizing yourself in your own living room. Find your own comfortable place to do your visualizations and have your "**Intention Chart**" (from earlier in this book) to focus on. Enjoy and trust the process.

Developing Skills for Visualizations

The following table helps you practice visualizing graphic details. There are no right or wrong answers— only YOUR answers.

Mental Imagery Table

Image to Recall	What you recalled	What you Missed
Example: Reflection of yourself in the mirror.	Example: Brown eyes; round face; heavy eyebrows; dark brown hair	Example: Small scar on left cheek; large forehead; small chin
Example: Speaking with someone on the phone.	Example: Deep voice; fast talker; monotone voice	Example: British accent; heavy nasal breathing
Example: You are tanning on a beach.	Example: Feel warmth of sun; feel warm sand on feet	Example: Feel and smell of sea breeze; taste of pineapple juice; hear the waves breaking on the shoreline; see birds flying above

Now do your own visualizing of details:

Image to Recall	What you recalled	What you Missed
Reflection of yourself in the mirror.		
Speaking with someone on the phone.		
Photo of significant other.		
Your car.		
Your living room.		

A picture is worth a thousand words but you can use whatever your most dominant sense is to your advantage when visualizing. Some people are more tuned into auditory memory and can remember a voice pattern more easily than a visual image. Others remember kinesthetically, or how something feels, including how emotional input makes them "feel." Increase your capacity to recall details and visualize using all of your senses.

Your subconscious mind acts as a filter, bringing details to your conscious awareness on a need-to-know basis as there is so much information streaming at you constantly. What you are aware of is what you focus on, so this can prevent you from seeing the bigger picture. Be aware of this mechanism that we all possess. Our reality is what we focus on and what we perceive it to be.

In this same fashion, we react to our perception of events, whether they happened in actual fact or not. Your brain cannot distinguish between a real event and a perceived event. In other words, your body responds to your mental images as if they were physically real. By making your visualizations as realistic as possible with clear positive intention, you will receive optimal results. You are recreating yourself in your new experience of wellness. Create your new healthy reality now. Remember that the energy of your intentions is actually being processed as new information within your body. That is the true power of visualization.

Why visualize? Visualization is a goal-oriented tool to help you specifically focus your ***attention*** while you take control of your ***intentions,*** synchronizing your conscious awareness with your subconscious beliefs. Visualizations bring this intention to life by getting all of your cells working together toward achieving this reality.

The mental imprint from visualizations sets off electrical charges in the neurons of your brain. Neuron connections are strengthened by repeated visualizations. With practice, you can create a permanent memory adjustment which influences your health or any other goal that you set your mind to. In healing, visualizations are tools to more closely align your intentions and thought patterns with your healing objective. Set what you desire in your conscious mind and then let your subconscious mind create as your intentions dictate.

For example, if you have a headache, your ***intention*** is for you to be pain free. A ***visualization*** would be sending step by step instructions to your body as to how this should be accomplished.

For instance:

- *Visualize the blood vessels in the area of the pain, opening and allowing unrestricted blood flow.*
- *Then visualize calming ripples of energy emanating from the area.*
- *Imagine every muscle in that area being totally relaxed.*

Through your ***focused intentions*** you can speed up the healing process with your visualizations.

Creating Your Goals

"The most important thing about goals is having one."
- Geoffry F. Abert

Your goals should be as clear, concise and specific as possible. The following **Goal Priority Table** exercise will help you to determine your focus.

- *Write down your goals and prioritize them, using a 1 to 10 rating scale.*
- *From this list select your top priority goal and address it first.*
- *State your goal as briefly and concisely as possible.*
- *Use the affirmation techniques in Section I which you have already learned, to help you stay mentally focused on your goals.*

If you have multiple health issues, focus on one specific goal for the first week, or until you are confident that you have made a change or succeeded in your objective. At the end of that week, use the **Goal Priority Table** to re-evaluate your goals and decide what your focus will be for the next week. This table may assist you in making your decision, as you rate your issues on a scale of 1 to 10.

Goal Priority Table

Priority	Goal	Baseline 1 to 10 Excellent to work required	Affirmation
1	Example: I want to be able to walk upstairs pain free	9	I enjoy walking upstairs effortlessly
2	Example: I want to have more energy	7	I enjoy walking briskly around my neighborhood
3	Example: I want to lose weight	6	I enjoy snacking on fruits and vegetables
1			
2			
3			

Basic Steps of a Visualization

"Try out your ideas by visualizing them in action."
- David Seabury

There are three steps for creating an anatomically accurate visualization:

1) Acquaint yourself with the area of concern (an anatomy book or internet sources)

2) Understand the mechanisms for the body healing itself (for example, lungs-coughing; kidney/bladder-clearing fluid; immune system)

3) Picture the body healed and functioning properly (for example, if pain is the issue, see yourself now as pain-free. If mobility is your challenge, visualize doing an activity that you love effortlessly and with ease.)

BE PROACTIVE: Take charge and learn everything there is to know about your health challenge. The more you understand about the process of regaining your wellness, the more accurate your visualizations will become. Your goal is to activate your own healing mechanisms as effectively as possible. Take responsibility, take charge, take action and be self-empowered.

Let's use an example to practice going through this three step process to form an anatomically accurate visualization. If, for instance, your challenge is a cold, know what a cold really is. All of us recognize when we have a cold. The challenge is to better understand the mechanisms involved so that we can more accurately visualize what is happening in the body.

EXAMPLE: STEP 1
Acquaint yourself with the area of concern:

With a quick search on the internet you can find out that a cold is a viral infection which affects the soft lining or mucous membrane of the nasal passages and throat. With a deeper search you can find out what a virus is, what the soft lining looks like, where exactly it is located in the nose and throat, etc....

Congested Nasal Passages

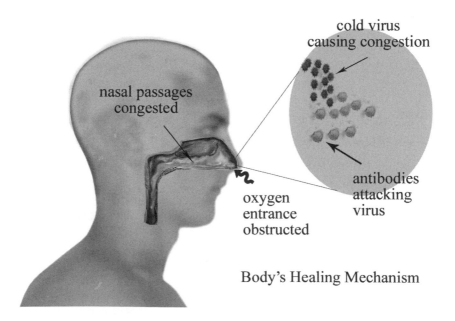

cold virus
causing congestion

nasal passages
congested

oxygen
entrance
obstructed

antibodies
attacking
virus

Body's Healing Mechanism

EXAMPLE: STEP 2
Understand the mechanisms for the body healing itself:

Once you have a clear picture of the anatomy of the area, focus on its functioning and how the body is going to heal the problem. Know the mechanisms that your body has for clearing your nasal passages and throat. Coughing and sneezing are helpful to remove congestion blockages and an active immune system should eventually recognize the virus which is causing the problem. Then your body will produce antibodies to neutralize the virus.

Visualizations stimulate your body's repairing of the area. With your understanding of the anatomy and healing mechanisms THEN you can begin to visualize. Direct your body in the process of healing itself. Imagine jump-starting these healing mechanisms to reduce congestion which is presently obstructing air passages making breathing a challenge. Direct your immune response to the virus causing the problem.

EXAMPLE: STEP 3
Picture the body healed and functioning properly:

Understand the healthy, ideal functioning of the area. Know what the healthy nasal passages and throat look like and their proper functioning. Watch the entire area working flawlessly with no sign of there ever being a problem. Whenever a negative thought creeps in about the healing,

- *STOP.*
- *CLEAR YOUR MIND by taking a deep breath in and out.*
- *THEN continue to visualize the area functioning in a perfect state until your mind is completely void of all negative thoughts.*

You can experiment with your own visualizations on a cold and see how effectively you are able to shorten the average time you have it. Usually a cold will last for a week to 10 days before the body's natural immune forces figure out what to do with this virus and get rid of it. Keep a journal and be encouraged by how you can effectively shorten the length of time needed to heal. You do not have to become an expert on colds. Just learn the basic steps so you can more accurately visualize how you will assist in your own healing from a cold, or any ailment.

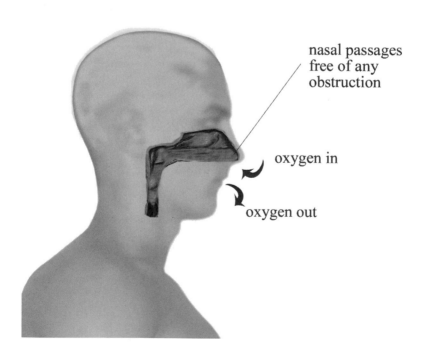

nasal passages
free of any
obstruction

oxygen in

oxygen out

Customizing Your Visualizations

"I visualize things in my mind before I have to do them. It's like having a mental workshop." - Jack Youngblood

It is important to thoroughly understand the previously discussed three basic steps involved in creating anatomically accurate visualizations before proceeding to the next level: ***creating your own customized visualizations***. Anatomically accurate visualizations can be customized by you and for you through the use of your own unique input. Everyone has a unique history and your visualizations should incorporate this. What is meaningful to you has an emotional impact which can strengthen your concentration on visualizations and their effectiveness.

Once you are comfortable with anatomically accurate visualizations, you can then begin to customize them. Integrate your own unique input of what resonates with you by using your memory of events, interests, hobbies, leisure activities and passions. You must find a visualization that feels right for you: this is your job. The material in this book will provide you with the tools you need to create the most effective visualizations for you. Your input is an essential part of this process.

It is usually easier to start your visualizations with anatomically accurate ones. During this process your mind will automatically start linking your visualizations to your recollection of experiences. For instance, if you love cooking, you may visualize progressing from step to step as you would by following instructions in a cookbook. A musician may hear changes and see images resonating in a musical sense. If you have ever seen balloons rising and drifting away in the wind, or watched ants building an anthill, these memories have meaning to you. Integrate these recollections into your customized visualizations to intensify the effects of your intentions on your unique healing journey.

Remember: Nobody knows YOU better than YOU.

During your visualizations you may find yourself drawn toward a specific area. In other words, things start happening which you did not intend to happen. No matter how unrelated to the actual problem it may seem, you must go with the flow. Listen as you are telling yourself something that you should investigate further. For instance, if you have a knee problem yet your focus keeps redirecting your thoughts to your hip, do not ignore these messages. Your hip may well be part of the issue and this is your body's way of alerting you to that connection.

There are no firm rules for visualizations as they vary between individuals. Modify your unique visualizations and explore them in order to find the ones which resonate best with your body and consequently your own health. You are the director of your own movie through the creation of your visualizations. Customize them to suit you. Create variations by referring to your **INTENTION CHART** as you experiment and decide what is most effective for you.

Visualizations for Self-Improvement

"If you think you can do a thing or think you can't do a thing, you're right." - Henry Ford

Many issues in your daily life can be improved through intention and visualization. We all constantly deal with stress, so visualizations help to control how you react to it. Explore how you can reach your peak performance in all your activities. A sound sleep is also something that many covet and is an attainable goal. Many of us would like to burn more body fat and improve body shape. Improve your physical stamina by focusing your intentions on exercise. An exercise regimen is attainable by everyone through visualizations. Of course you can use these techniques to visualize your next day. Be proactive and take charge of every aspect of your life!

Managing Stress

Recall my discussion of how DNA responds to environmental factors. A recent study demonstrated that the coiling of DNA can be altered by being exposed to different emotions. When researchers exposed DNA to a high level of frustration, an increase in winding of the DNA resulted. Its coiling actually tightened under this stress. When researchers focused loving intentions toward the DNA, it actually relaxed and lengthened. DNA would change its coiling according to the emotions that were felt by the researchers in the experiments. (R. McCraty, G.Rein, et al.(2003). "Modulation of DNA Conformation by Heart-Focused Intention" HeartMath Research.)

I predict that it will be proven that the DNA is responding to the light energy frequency emitted from emotions being created by our intentions. Using this same mechanism, our immune systems can be enhanced or depressed depending on our intentions. We are both the transmitter and receiver from the field of information.

Visualization for managing stress:

Relaxing Your DNA

This visualization is helpful to anyone at anytime. It can be used in any situation as a stress management tool, an immune system booster or energy enhancer, as it involves every cell in your body. While breathing, relaxing and intending to send love to your DNA, see the strands of DNA relaxing, lengthening and unwinding. Remember that DNA is located in every cell in your body.

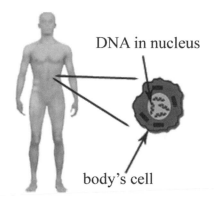

DNA in nucleus

body's cell

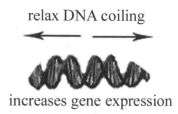

relax DNA coiling

increases gene expression

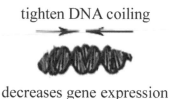

tighten DNA coiling

decreases gene expression

- *Imagine all the energy of the universe circling above your head, available for your use.*
- *Feel, see and know that you are surrounded by intense pure healing energy. Your intention is to send love to all of your cells and relax your DNA, thus stimulating your immune system.*
- *With inhalation, bring in universal energy and collect it in your heart.*
- *With exhalation, imagine sending the energy from your heart radiating into your arms to your fingertips.*
- *Place your fingertips on your heart area and inhale this energy flow to your heart. Continue to imagine this flow as an energy circuit; from your heart through your entire body and returning to your heart.*
- *Imagine every DNA strand as a coiled magnet, attracting and absorbing energy which relaxes and uncoils the DNA.*

- *Focus on an individual DNA strand and project this image in front of you. See clearly the entire process in this one image of the DNA strand. THEN shift your focus to knowing that this is happening to all DNA in your body simultaneously.*

Then customize your own visualizations:

- *See the DNA strand in every cell in its relaxed state become so full of loving light that it starts radiating its own light.*
- *Imagine all of your DNA resonating at the same frequency, as does the harmonious light of your focused intention. All of your individual cells reach a similar frequency, until they are all resonating at the same coherent vibration. You are so alive with light energy that, if you look in a mirror, your aura will be almost too bright to see your reflection.*

A variation on this visualization could be:

- *Visualize your entire body as a guitar resonating with a single harmonious chord strummed in perfect tune.*
- *When your entire body resonates in harmony with your intentions, you no longer see every DNA strand as emanating an individual light but the entire body as one continuous harmonious light. Every strand of DNA in your body is now aware of your intentions and it relaxes accordingly.*

SEE your entire being light up with focused intentions.
FEEL your harmonic flow of energy.
HEAR your single resonating frequency.
MAKE IT REAL.

Fat Burner Visualization

This is an excellent visualization to keep yourself in physical shape. It can be used no matter where you are on the weigh scale. Of course you must give serious consideration to your diet and exercise regimen. This visualization may give you the edge that you need to stay focused, motivated and inspired in your fitness and dieting program.

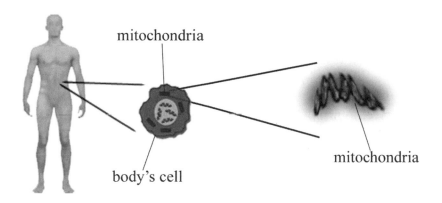

mitochondria

body's cell

mitochondria

- *Focus on your body area where you want fat burning to occur.*
- *Visualize all of the undesired fat moving to the mitochondria in that area. Mitochondria are organelles that are present within every cell and supply the cells with energy.*
- *Focus on an individual mitochondria and project this image in front of you.*
- *See clearly the entire fat burning process in this one image of the mitochondrion. THEN shift your focus to knowing that this is happening to all cells in your body simultaneously.*
- *Visualize the fat in every cell being broken down within the mitochondria and the fat cells shrinking as a result of this. The*

131

fat is metabolized in the body, giving you increased energy.

- *Imagine attracting more fat to the mitochondria where it will be metabolized.*
- *At the same time as you are doing this visualization, physically tighten your muscles in the area you are focussing on. For instance, if you are focussing on burning abdominal fat, physically pull in your abdominal muscles in synch with your visualization.*
- *In your mind's eye imagine yourself thinner without any weight issues.*
- *With the increase in your energy, see yourself doing activities which you would like to participate in.*
- *Build your confidence knowing that this new you is your future.*

Then customize your own visualizations:

- *Start visualizing using the anatomically correct version until you understand the process.*
- *As with any visualization, you can stylize or modify it to whatever you feel works for you. Let your mind wander and pay attention to what you come up with to express yourself.*
- *You might customize your visualization be using velcro-coated molecules which cause the fat to stick to them and dispose of them in your internal furnace which burns fuel (fat) for useful energy.*
- *Another example might be picturing ants gathering up the excess fat molecules and eating away at them and disposing of the waste products through your own disposal mechanism by-products of urine and feces.*

SEE yourself as you want to look.
FEEL yourself energized in your improved physical self.
HEAR your frequency resonating with pride.
MAKE IT REAL.

Visualization for Better Sleep

> *"A good laugh and a long sleep are the best cures*
> *in the doctor's book." - Irish proverb*

You can create a visualization to increase your body's own mechanisms to enhance sleep. Melatonin which is a biochemical produced in the pineal gland located near the pituitary and hypothalamus glands in the brain, facilitates sleep.

Natural Melatonin for Sleep

pineal gland

melatonin release

- *Have a clear picture in your mind of where the pineal gland is located and what it looks like.*
- *Light is thought to suppress the production of melatonin. Visualize absolutely no light signals reaching the pineal gland through your eyes.*
- *Visualize the gland as a mini-factory pumping out the sleep-enhancing chemical melatonin.*

- *See your body receiving these biochemical signals to promote sleep.*
- *In your mind's eye imagine yourself in a deep sleep with no thoughts in your awareness whatsoever.*

Then customize your own visualizations:

- *As with any visualization, you can stylize or modify it to whatever you feel works for you. Let your mind wander and pay attention to what you come up with.*
- *For example, variations on this visualization might include seeing or feeling the melatonin as microscopic soft pillows being released in between all of your stressed out and over-worked neurons. This cushions your brain and softens the worry load in your brain.*
- *Another variation might be to hear a calming tone resonating and emanating from your brain. See the melatonin as soft, radiating light which is flushing out all of your worries and coating your brain with sleep softeners.*

SEE yourself sleeping soundly.
FEEL yourself melting into your soft pillow.
HEAR yourself breathing rhythmically.
MAKE IT REAL.

Anxiety or Panic Attacks

"I've had thousands of problems in my life, most of which never actually happened." - Mark Twain

- *Picture yourself in a situation that you would usually try desperately to avoid for fear of a panic attack.*
- *Imagine breathing in relaxing, calming light.*
- *See soft, gentle light radiating from your lungs to your brain, flooding your brain with light, washing away your worries.*
- *Imagine soft pillows being released with the light, cushioning and protecting your brain.*
- *Hear a calming tone resonating and emanating from your brain.*
- *See every cell in your body remain perfectly calm and relaxed.*

You are relaxed, calm and in full control of your environment and circumstances as you take charge of the situation.

Visualization for Exercise

Everyone benefits from exercise, from professional athletes to the physically challenged. Exercise stimulates your entire system, from increased oxygen exchange to secretion of hormones. Having a regular exercise program is important and almost everyone is capable of participating to some degree. A visualization of exercise promotes more efficient cellular activity. This sends messages from your mind to your body that you are optimizing your physical health. Even small changes send signals to every cell that changes are being made.

A physically fit person should visualize themselves achieving the ultimate goal in their exercise routine. For instance, a competitive marathon runner visualizes crossing the finish line first in an effortless gliding stride. Use all your senses. Imagine it to be a hot day with the sun beating down, challenging your energy resources. Feel your sweat dripping off your face, neck and back. Hear the echo of other runners close to you. SEE IT, FEEL IT, HEAR IT; MAKE IT REAL. In spite of all these obstacles and distractions you still sprint across the finish line first, with energy to spare.

Once I had a vivid dream of exercising only my biceps, using every biceps exercise possible. When I awoke the next morning my biceps were incredibly sore, as if I had an intense work-out. My body did not know the difference between visualizing this exercise and the physical exercise itself. That is what you are trying to achieve by doing exercise visualizations.

It is important to view physical activity from the perspective of what you *can* do rather than what you *cannot* do. If you are only able to bend one toe, then *DO IT*! And regularly. *Visualize* bending the rest of your toes until this too becomes your reality.

SEE yourself energized by your exercise routine.
FEEL the flow of oxygen within every re-energized cell.
HEAR your own harmonic flow of energy through your entire being.
MAKE IT REAL.

Visualization for Mental Acuity

Improve your efficiency in every aspect of your life by fine-tuning the sending and receiving of information beyond your five senses. Clearly send and receive what your focused intention is. Tune in!

You can create a visualization to increase your body's own mechanisms to enhance your mental acuity. This is particularly useful for those big stressor moments in life, such as writing exams, job interviews and doing presentations in front of people. I use it frequently and find it very helpful.

- *Have a clear picture in your mind of the neurons in your brain.*
- *Imagine or hum aloud a tone (like humm) and see all of your neurons vibrating to that same tone.*
- *Once this resonance is in focus, light up all of your pathways. It may help to think of calming lightning bolts supplying you with the energy needed to do this.*
- *Imagine these neurons growing outward as they become like tentacles reaching out far beyond your physical self.*
- *See the tentacles tuning in to information you need in this field of information.*
- *Attach and connect your tentacles to what information you seek and pull it into you, allowing it to become part of your awareness.*

Then customize your own visualizations:

- *As with any visualization, you can stylize or modify it to whatever you feel works for you. Let your mind wander and pay attention to what you come up with.*
- *For example, variations on this visualization might include seeing or feeling the tentacles as roots of a plant growing downward and outward, connecting with what you seek.*
- *Another variation is seeing your own light radiate out and connect to what you need to know.*
- *You may hear a calming tone resonating and emanating from your brain which resonates at the same frequency as the information you seek.*
- *See velcro-coated tentacles sticking to what information you need to know. **Become one with it: that's tuning in.***

Slowing the Aging Process

Why do we age? How can we influence this process of aging? Until recently the answers to these questions were a mystery. We now know that the primary factor determining age is the accumulation of oxidative damage. Throughout our entire lifetime, proteins within the cells are affected by free radicals. Damaged proteins accumulate as protein aggregates which cause a variety of age related defects to the cells.

These unwanted proteins are removed by a natural process in which a double membrane structure surrounds this region within the cell. This structure then fuses with a lysosome which is the equivalent of the cell's garbage disposal unit where its contents are digested, thus removing waste from the cell. In our youth, this process occurs at a faster rate, so age-related defects do not occur as quickly.

In other organisms, scientists have manipulated the genes to make it happen more frequently. As a result, the average lifespan of these organisms was greatly increased, sometimes to twice the length of their normal lifespan. (Simonsen, A.et al. (2008) "Promoting basal levels of autophagy in the nervous system." *Autophagy* 4:2, 176-184)

We are still a long way from having an effective means of controlling this process because there is much that is not understood. Use your *intentions* and *visualizations* to slow the effects of aging.

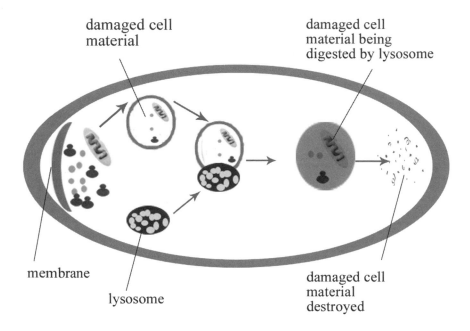

- *Visualize all the damaged proteins collecting in one area of the cell.*
- *See this collection of damaged material being enveloped by a membrane as seen in the above drawing which isolates its contents from the rest of the cell.*
- *Visualize this membrane structure full of damaged proteins fusing with a lysosome.*
- *See the lysosome digest the damaged protein structure, leaving the rest of the cell intact.*
- *Focus on an individual cell and project this image in front of you. See clearly the entire process occurring in this one image of the cell. THEN shift your focus to knowing that this is happening to all cells in your body.*

Specific Health Challenges

Now that you are familiar with the process of creating anatomically accurate visualizations and customizing them, you are ready to create visualizations for specific health challenges.

Create a table for your health challenge, such as you see on the following pages which includes:

- What needs healing
- Possible causes or risk factors
- Anatomy of the problem area
- Symptoms
- Body's mechanism for healing

From this table establish your goals for healing visualizations and prioritize them so you can address them one at a time.

- Create anatomically accurate visualizations.
- THEN customize them with your own memories, hobbies, passions, experiences.
- Find what resonates with you.
- Keep this process interesting by experimenting with variations of your visualizations, so as not to bore yourself.

The DVD "Visualizations for Self-Empowerment" provides dynamic visualizations which you may find very useful for creatively customizing your own visualizations. Remember that no matter how unusual your visualizations may seem, it is your intentions that heal. You are not going to have a negative result from a positive intent. Visualizations activate and stimulate your body's own healing mechanisms.

In this section many health conditions are used to demonstrate how you can create visualizations. If your issue is not specifically listed, it is important to understand that the PROCESS is the same for every condition. Use this section as a guide to adapt to your individual needs.

Fibromyalgia and Chronic Fatigue Syndrome

Fibromyalgia is widespread pain, stiffness and tenderness of the muscles, tendons and joints. Many people with fibromyalgia have difficulty sleeping and awaken feeling tired, rather than refreshed. Although fibromyalgia is common, its cause is unknown.

Chronic Fatigue Syndrome is also a poorly understood debilitating disorder sharing many similar symptoms to fibromyalgia. These can include pain and sleep issues, cognitive difficulties, mental and physical exhaustion.

The following table describes possible risk factors of fibromyalgia and chronic fatigue syndrome, anatomy of the problem area and the body's own mechanisms for healing. This table indicates the type of information you should collect before creating visualizations.

Fibromyalgia and Chronic Fatigue Syndrome Table

What needs healing	Fibromyalgia and chronic fatigue syndrome
Possible causes or risk factors	• Trauma or injury • Disturbed sleep patterns • Infection • Nervous system abnormalities
Anatomy of problem area	Joints, muscles, ligaments, tendons, nervous system
Symptoms	Swelling; pain; severe fatigue
Body's mechanisms for healing	• Remove swelling from joints • Decrease level of neural transmitters (pain signals) • Increase serotonin levels for sleep (see previous Visualizations for Better Sleep)
Typical tender points for fibromyalgia	

Creating specific visualizations to enhance healing mechanisms for fibromyalgia and chronic fatigue syndrome encompass three major areas of concern and therefore the goals for healing are:

- Remove swelling from joints
- Decrease pain and relax muscles and joints
- Increase the body's natural chemical levels for sleep (Refer to previous Visualization for Better Sleep)

Swelling (four different sample visualizations)

Fluid Removal Visualization #1:

You can create a useful visualization to remove swelling from a localized area by imagining a needle injected into your area of swelling, for instance your ankle joint.

- *Imagine injecting an empty syringe into your joint, then pulling back on the syringe, extracting out all of your unnecessary fluid from your joint.*
- *Visualize filling the syringe and dispose of it by dissipating it into a black hole.*
- *In your mind's eye FEEL that the swelling is decreasing.*
- *Repeat this procedure several times, until you feel that the fluid has all been energetically removed.*
- *KNOW that your intentions are influencing your healing.*

Visualizations

Fluid Removal Visualization #2:

- *Imagine vacuuming all of the unnecessary fluid that surrounds your joint.*
- *Visualize filling the vacuum bag and then emptying the fluid into the universe.*
- *Repeat this procedure several times, until you feel that the fluid has all been energetically removed.*
- *In your mind's eye FEEL that the swelling is decreasing.*
- *KNOW that your intentions are influencing your healing.*

Fluid Removal Visualization #3:

- *Imagine using an absorbent cloth to absorb the fluid retained in your joint, energetically absorbing fluid until the cloth is saturated.*
- *Wring out the fluid and dispose of it by watching it dissipate into the universe.*
- *In your mind's eye FEEL that the swelling is decreasing.*
- *Repeat this procedure several times, until you feel that the fluid has all been energetically removed.*
- *KNOW that your intentions are influencing your healing.*

Fluid Removal Visualization #4:

Use your body's own mechanisms to eliminate unwanted fluid:

- *Every time you eliminate body waste through urination, bowel movements or sweating, visualize the excess fluid from your joint being eliminated from your body.*

- *In your mind's eye FEEL that the swelling is decreasing.*
- *See this happening regularly and establish this routine.*
- *KNOW that your intentions are influencing your healing.*

Use any of these visualizations, one at a time or in any combination. You will quickly get a sense of which visualizations are most productive for you: what resonates with you. Your own memories are your best resource for customizing your visualizations. Feel free to create visualizations that only have significant meaning to you.

Pain

Pain signals are intense and chaotic. Your goal is to calm the impulses down. Keep in mind that every cell essentially has its own memory and through your visualizations you are simply telling each cell to release the memory of pain. Muscle relaxation is a key here. Imagine relaxing your muscles as you do any visualizations. Basic steps for a pain visualization are:

- *See the area where your pain issue is.*
- *Breathe in light energy and radiate this calming energy to the source of your pain.*
- *In your mind, see the light reducing the amplitude of the nerve impulses until there are only calming ripples in the previously painful area which gradually diminish and disappear.*

An alternative visualization might be using carbonated water in the nerves to dissipate and release the pain signal. A dial may be used to actually turn down the intensity of the pain signal.

Change your perception of the pain. Use your creativity.

Many visualizations in my "Visualization for Self-Empowerment" DVD can be used for pain issues, including fibromyalgia. I highly recommend that you review using them as well, as they will not be repeated in this book. The Light Injections visualization and Lightning Bolt visualization are both very helpful for addressing pain issues and are both covered in the DVD.

Multiple Sclerosis

Multiple Sclerosis (MS) is a common disease of the brain and spinal cord or central nervous system (CNS). Nerve cells are responsible for transmitting communication signals both within the CNS and between the CNS and the rest of the body. MS causes inflammation called plaques or lesions and at these locations the nerve insulating material (myelin) is damaged.

The following table describes possible risk factors of multiple sclerosis, anatomy of the problem area, symptoms and the body's own mechanisms for healing. This table indicates the type of information you should collect before creating your visualizations for multiple sclerosis.

Multiple Sclerosis Table

What needs healing	Multiple Sclerosis
Possible causes or risk factors	Unknown cause but risk factors may include exposure to viruses, trauma and heavy metals (toxins).
Anatomy of problem area	MS is a chronic, unpredictable neurological disease that affects the central nervous system including the brain, spinal cord and optic nerves. MS causes damage to myelin which is the fatty substance surrounding nerve fibers that acts as an insulator. Myelin damage impairs the nerve's ability to conduct electrical impulses to and from the brain. This produces the symptoms of MS.
Symptoms	Symptoms include problems with visual, motor, sensory, coordination, balance, bowel, bladder, sexual and cognitive functions and systems.
Body's mechanisms for healing	MS is an electrical insulation problem. The current is disrupted- hence the signal received is missed or inaccurate information is received. Remyelination is the goal for any healing.

Visualization for remyelination:

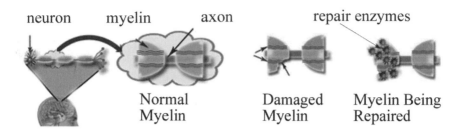

neuron	myelin	axon		repair enzymes

Normal Myelin

Damaged Myelin

Myelin Being Repaired

- *Imagine that you are producing an enzyme which promotes remyelination for the rebuilding of your damaged areas.*
- *Be creative; visualize long strands of myelin which you knit or sew over to replace the damaged myelin.*
- *Imagine creating a sleeve to place over this area, similar to those used to hold a collection of wires together.*
- *Patch the myelin by wrapping the damaged areas with tape.*
- *Imagine a nerve impulse travelling unimpeded from one nerve cell to the next. See the intact myelin allowing this to happen.*
- *You are in complete control of the messages being sent from your nervous system to all other areas of your body. See this happening with laser precision.*
- *All the synapses of your brain are firing, sending intense pulses of energy down your spine, branching out until they reach the smallest nerve endings. Feel and see this happening. You are reconnected and functioning properly.*
- *KNOW that your intentions are influencing your healing.*

Lightning bolt grounded to the center of the Earth visualization:

This visualization combines the lightning bolt visualization from the DVD with grounding your energy to the center of the Earth, like tree roots. Lightning bolt visualizations stimulate your nervous system by sending electrical energy to every part of you. Many people with MS have balance and vertigo issues. Grounding this energy into the center of the Earth roots your feet, creating balance and a steadier stance. You can do this visualization standing, sitting or lying down; just make sure you are rooting the lightning bolts and yourself to the center of the Earth.

Use this visualization to regain physical energy, vitality and strength. Your nervous system has become overloaded. This visualization forces your body to reboot and restore your healthy state.

- *Imagine that lightning strikes the top of your head.*
- *Your entire nervous system lights up as the electrical energy spreads through your body.*
- *Intense pulses of energy rush down your spine, branching out until they reach the smallest nerve endings.*
- *Ground the lightning bolts by directing them through the soles of your feet to the center of the Earth. Be a lightning rod, in total control of guiding the energy.*
- *See yourself energized and rooted into the Earth. This is where you belong so feel comfortable in your steady stance.*
- *Gradually lessen the intensity of the lightning, as this lightning storm passes. Imagine calming ripples being emitted from your entire nervous system, as you connect to the center of the Earth.*

Visualizations

- *Practice this visualization using various colors and intensities. For instance for a more gentle approach, try pink lightning bolts rippling gently as they connect to all of your nerve endings. See the impulses move without any hindrance.*
- *In your mind's eye FEEL that you are in control of the connection to the lightning energy throughout your body. Feel control, comfort and confidence in your balance and stance as you ground energy through your feet to the center of the Earth. Be connected.*
- *KNOW that your intentions are influencing your healing.*

SEE the intense light of the lightning bolt.
FEEL the energy ripping through you as you
ground to the Earth's center.
HEAR its thunder.
SMELL and TASTE its electrical charge.
MAKE IT REAL.

Tinnitus

Tinnitus is sound or noise originating within one or both ears, rather than from the external environment. Descriptions of the noise vary from a ringing, buzzing, whistling or humming. There are several known causes of its occurrence, as noted in the information table below.

Tinnitus Table

What needs healing	The areas that we will be focusing our visualization on are the vestibular, cochlear and auditory nerves.
Possible causes or risk factors	Tinnitus can be caused by an ear infection, extreme loud noise, impaction of ear wax, ototoxic-chemicals, including some medications and other conditions.
Anatomy of problem area	Varies and requires your research.
Symptoms	Tinnitus is a symptom described as the perception of sound without a corresponding external source.
Body's mechanisms for healing	Control of over-active neurons in the ear. Restore proper functioning of the cochlear, vestibular and auditory nerves.

Tinnitus Visualization:

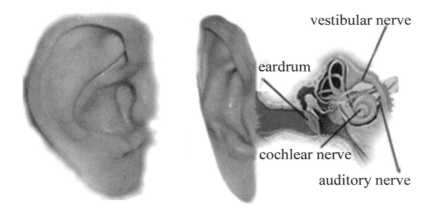

- *Find yourself a quiet place to focus on your visualizations.*
- *Focus your mind on the location of the vestibular, cochlear and auditory nerves.*
- *In your mind's eye see calming ripples travelling along the vestibular nerve as shown in the previous sketch.*
- *Switch your visualization to the cochlear nerve with the same calming ripples.*
- *See the hairs in the cochlea being perfectly still, yet flexible and fluid.*
- *At the same time, see the auditory nerve conducting the sound wave and imagine turning down the volume control on any disturbing sounds, gradually reducing to nothing.*
- *Repeat this routine several times a day and record your level of progress. Use a grading scale to monitor your improvement. On a scale of 1 to 10, let 10 be very loud and 1 is nearly inaudible. Turn it down!*
- *KNOW that your intentions are influencing your healing.*

Diabetes

Diabetes is a condition which affects the body by not producing enough insulin or improperly using it. Insulin is a hormone
essential for the conversion of sugar, starches and other food into energy. Insulin takes the sugar, or glucose, from the blood into the cells.
Although the cause of diabetes is uncertain, lifestyle risk factors such
as obesity and lack of exercise often appear to be involved, particularly
in Type II.

In Type I diabetes, formerly known as juvenile diabetes, the
body does not produce enough insulin. The goal is to see the pancreas
repair itself to become a healthy, functioning organ that provides suf-
ficient insulin. The primary focus of this section is the more common
TYPE II, where either the body under-produces insulin or insulin is
inadequately used by the cells.

With diabetes, glucose builds up in the blood instead of being
processed into the cells. Immediately your cells may be starved for
energy. Complications of diabetes caused by high blood glucose levels may include heart disease, blindness, nerve and kidney damage.

Type II Diabetes Table

What needs healing	Diabetes Type II Instead of sugar (glucose) moving into your cells, sugar builds up in your bloodstream. This occurs when your pancreas doesn't make enough insulin or your cells become resistant to the action of insulin.
Possible causes or risk factors	Exactly why this happens is uncertain, although excess fat, especially abdominal fat and inactivity seem to be important risk factors.
Anatomy of problem area	Type II diabetes, once known as adult-onset or non insulin-dependent diabetes, is a chronic condition that affects the way your body metabolizes sugar (glucose), your body's main source of fuel. Type II diabetes is often preventable but the condition is on the rise, fueled largely by the current obesity epidemic and more sedentary lifestyles.
Symptoms	Fatigue; frequent urination; unusual thirst
Body's mechanisms for healing	Producing and recognizing the insulin for proper use in the body.

Diabetes Visualization:

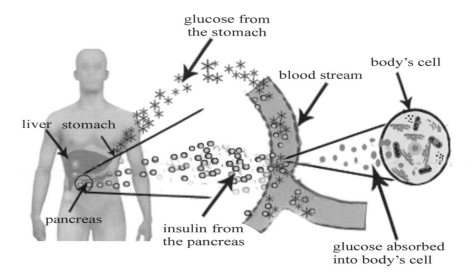

- *Find yourself a quiet place to focus on your visualizations.*
- *Focus your mind on the location of the pancreas, where insulin is produced.*
- *In your mind's eye visualize insulin being created and recognized by your body.*
- *See insulin in your blood attracting sugar. Insulin and sugar are attached and permeate the cell membrane, taking this energy into your cells.*

Then customize your own visualizations:

- *See this energy as light which lights up all of your cells.*
- *Radiate the light out from your cells, sending calming ripples of energy travelling throughout your body.*

- *Feel and see your newfound energy as your body re-energizes itself, bathing in this light.*
- *Focus on an individual cell and project this image in front of you. Visualize the process happening to one cell. THEN shift your focus to knowing that this is happening to all cells in your body simultaneously.*
- *Change your visualizations by imagining insulin as metallic and attracting sugar magnetically- or as velcro and attaching to fabric. Be creative.*
- *Repeat this routine often throughout your day and record your level of progress. Use a grading scale to monitor your improvement.*
- *KNOW that your intentions are influencing your healing.*

Regulating Biochemicals in the Body

DNA is found in the nucleus of every cell in our body. Proteins and enzymes are produced from this information which assist with all of our bodily functions.

It is fairly common for people to receive test results indicating that a biochemical in the body is either elevated or below normal range. The prefix "hypo" means less than which in medical terms denotes a deficiency in the biochemical level. Examples of this are: low thyroid levels, or hypo-thyroid and low glucose levels, or hypoglycemia. They usually require increasing biochemical output to reach the "normal" levels, or up-regulating.

The prefix "hyper" means above, as there is an excessive amount of a given biochemical produced in the body. Examples of this are: high thyroid levels or hyper-thyroid and high glucose levels, or hyperglycemia. They usually require decreasing biochemical output to reach the "normal" levels, or down-regulating.

The following tables and visualizations can be used to assist with your healing process.

Biochemical Up-Regulating Table

What needs healing	Hypo- conditions: the body usually requires stimulating to increase biochemical levels.
Possible causes or risk factors	Varies depending on what the condition is and which gland is involved. In many cases the gland is simply under-producing the necessary level.
Anatomy of problem area	Varies and requires your research. The pituitary, hypothalamus and pineal glands are important biochemical factories in the body.
Symptoms	Symptoms vary since there are many conditions which fall under the umbrella of hypo. Your healthcare professional can best advise you regarding the necessary testing.
Body's mechanisms for healing	The body must signal the gland to produce more of the deficient biochemical. On the genetic level, the DNA plays a major role in the production of proteins and enzymes necessary for glands to produce the proper levels of biochemicals in the body.

Genetic Visualization to Increase Chemical Processes:

Increase (up-regulate) Chemical Process

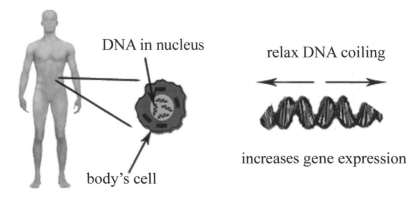

DNA in nucleus

relax DNA coiling

body's cell

increases gene expression

- *Focus your mind on the location of the gland or body area of concern.*
- *In your mind's eye see the DNA in the cells relax and unwind as shown in the sketch above.*
- *See that when DNA is relaxed, more proteins are produced, stimulating the gland or area being worked on.*
- *Focus on an individual DNA strand and project this image in front of you. Visualize the process happening to one DNA strand. THEN shift your focus to knowing that this is happening to all DNA in your body simultaneously.*

Then customize your own visualizations:

- *Visualize calming pulses of energy moving through the gland which stimulate your immune system to focus more effectively.*
- *Visualize a stronger immune presence in the area and more importantly, see your immune system more effectively recognizing the problem.*
- *KNOW that your intentions are influencing your healing.*

Biochemical Down-Regulating Table

What needs healing	Hyper- conditions: the body usually requires reduction of biochemical levels
Possible causes or risk factors	Varies depending on what the condition is and which gland is involved. In many cases the gland is simply over-producing the necessary level.
Anatomy of problem area	Varies and requires your research. The pituitary, hypothalamus and pineal glands are important biochemical factories in the body.
Symptoms	Symptoms vary since there are many conditions which fall under the umbrella of hyper. Your healthcare professional can best advise you regarding the necessary testing.
Body's mechanisms for healing	The body must signal the gland to produce less of the excess biochemical. On the genetic level, the DNA plays a major role in the production of proteins and enzymes necessary for glands to produce the proper levels of biochemicals in the body.

Visualizations

Genetic Visualization to Decrease Chemical Processes:

Decrease (down-regulate) Chemical Processes

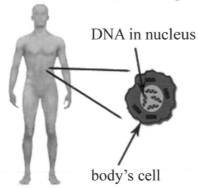

DNA in nucleus

body's cell

tighten DNA coiling

decreases gene expression

- *Focus your mind on the location of the gland or body area of concern.*
- *In your mind's eye see the coiling of the DNA tighten in the cells as shown in the preceding sketch.*
- *Know that when the DNA is tightly coiled, fewer proteins are produced which in turn produce fewer biochemicals.*
- *Focus on an individual DNA strand and project this image in front of you. Visualize the process happening to one DNA strand. THEN shift your focus to knowing that this is happening to all DNA in your body simultaneously.*
- *KNOW that your intentions are influencing your healing.*

Cancer

Cancer is uncontrolled growth of a group of cells which may invade and spread to other locations in the body. It is believed that every person has some cancer cells within their body. When your immune system is functioning properly, your body is able to prevent these cancer cells from forming tumors. For this reason, it is important to keep your immune system functioning at its optimum level. Addressing your external influences, such as diet and exercise and your internal influences, such as how you react to stress, are all variables which are within your control.

The following table describes possible risk factors for cancer, anatomy of the problem area and the body's own mechanisms for healing. This table indicates the type of information you should collect before beginning visualizations for any cancer. Consult your healthcare practitioner as early detection is beneficial. As always, any of the visualizations can be used in conjunction with any medical treatment.

General Cancer Table

Possible causes or risk factors	• Stress • Diet • Lifestyle habits (i.e. smoking) • Lack of exercise • Environment
Anatomy of problem area	Cancer can occur in any part of the body. Cells become abnormal and continue to divide and form cells more quickly than normal cells.
Body's mechanisms for healing	The immune system is the control center for our body's defenses. If there is a disturbance (i.e. cancer) in the body, our immune system produces a cascade of biochemical activity to fight the cancer.

The following are general visualizations which can be used for all types of cancer. They can be used in any order and in any combination:

Wringing out Tumor Visualization #1:

Dr. Edgar Mitchell, the Apollo astronaut and IONS scientist, successfully used this visualization in conjunction with distant healing, for a cancerous tumor in his kidney which is no longer present.

- *Visualize wringing out the tumor in order to dry out all of the vascular connections supplying blood to the tumor.*
- *Every time that you do this visualization, see the tumor getting smaller and the cancer dying off.*
- *See and know in your mind that this visualization is encouraging your body to more effectively fight off the problem.*
- *KNOW that your intentions are influencing your healing.*

Isolating Tumor Visualization #2:

Cancer cells can break loose from a tumor and travel through the bloodstream or the lymphatic system. Using visualizations to break down communications within a tumor is helpful, as the cancer cells pass on the message to all the cells in the tumor in a domino effect. Your goal is to create disorganization and disharmony within the cells of the tumor, causing a communication breakdown.

- *Visualize the location of your primary tumor i.e. breast, lung etc.*
- *Move your focused intention to that area.*
- *With inhalation, breathe in healing energy to your focused area.*
- *Surround the tumor with a hard, impervious shell which effectively cuts off the communications between the tumor and the surrounding tissues.*
- *See the primary tumor unable to communicate with other potential cancer cells, as you have disabled the cancer's communication system.*
- *Visualize and SEE the tumor dying off as it is unable to communicate effectively.*
- *KNOW that your intentions are influencing your healing.*

Cellular Level Visualization #3:

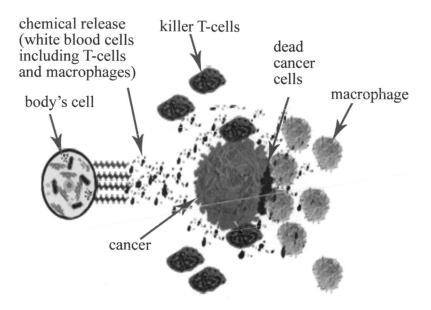

chemical release (white blood cells including T-cells and macrophages)

killer T-cells

dead cancer cells

macrophage

body's cell

cancer

- *Focus your mind on the cancer location.*
- *In your mind's eye see every cell in your body releasing a chemical which surrounds the tumor.*
- *Know that this chemical attracts (like a magnet) a variety of white blood cells including killer T-cells and macrophages to the area of the tumor.*
- *The killer T-cells release toxins locally in very high concentrations that kill the cancer cells.*
- *See the macrophages eat away at the dead cancer cells.*
- *KNOW that your intentions are influencing your healing.*

Cutting Off Blood Supply to Tumor Visualization #4:

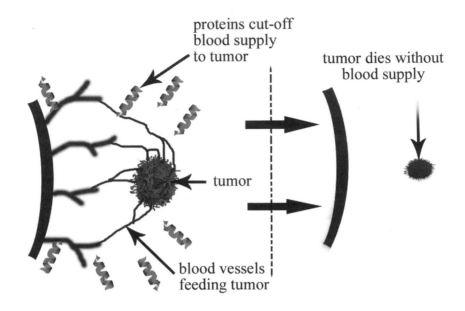

- *Focus your mind on the cancer location.*
- *In your mind's eye see razor-sharp proteins attracted to the location of the tumor, like iron filings to a magnet.*
- *See these razor-sharp proteins attaching to every blood vessel feeding the tumor, essentially cutting off the blood supply of the tumor.*
- *Visualize the tumor shrivelling up and dying as it starves without nourishment.*
- *KNOW that your intentions are influencing your healing.*

Many visualizations in the DVD "***Visualization for Self-Empowerment***" can be used for cancer. I highly recommend that you review them, as they will not be repeated in this manual. Fire Visualization, Smart Energy Packets (SEPs), Explosions and White Blood Cell visualizations are very helpful for addressing cancer issues and all are covered in the DVD.

Specific Cancers

If you have a specific cancer issue, it is helpful to create a table of information. The following examples show the format which can be used for any challenge. Many of the same visualization techniques can be used interchangeably with any cancer. Keep in mind that your own personal life experiences and memories should be used to help you customize your specific visualizations. This will give the visualizations more meaning and emotional impact for your benefit.

The most common form of cancer in adults is skin cancer. Breast, lung, pancreatic, prostate and colorectal cancers will also be addressed in this chapter.

1) Breast Cancer Table

Possible causes or risk factors	• Diet: Risk increases with high intake of fat in diet. • Smoking increases the risk of breast cancer. • Exercise reduces the risk of developing breast cancer. • Alcohol: excessive consumption increases the risk of developing breast cancer.
Anatomy of problem area	Breast tissue extends from just below the collarbone to the 7th rib and from the breastbone to the underarm area, including about 20 ducts.
Symptoms	May include lump in the breast, changes in size or shape of breast or nipple, discharge from nipple.
Body's mechanism for healing	Like all cancers, it is important to get your body to recognize this area as a problem requiring your attention and focus. Create more specific visualizations using previous concepts.
	Breast lymph node artery fatty tissue lobule duct nipple

2) Lung Cancer Table

Possible causes or risk factors	• Smoking • Excessive exposure to radon gas • Air Pollution: Excessive exposure to asbestos, paints, diesel exhaust, herbicides and insecticides.
Anatomy of problem area	Lungs are a pair of cone-shaped organs which expand and contract through breathing as they take in oxygen from the air. Every cell requires oxygen to carry out its normal functions. The lungs, located in the chest, are made of spongy, pinkish-gray tissue and are enveloped by a membrane called the pleura.
Symptoms	May include chronic cough, coughing up blood in phlegm, shortness of breath or pain when breathing.
Body's mechanism for healing	Like all cancers, it is important to get your body to recognize this area as a problem requiring your attention and focus. Create more specific visualizations using previous concepts.

3) Skin Cancer Table

Possible causes or risk factors	• Excess exposure to sunlight • Excessive exposure to tanning salon lights.
Anatomy of problem area	Skin cancer is a malignant growth of the skin. It is the most common form of cancer and the most curable. The most common form is non-melanoma which is very treatable. The least common is melanoma which is more serious.
Symptoms	May include a spot or sore that is itchy, changing in color or size, painful, bleeding, is slow to heal or does not heal.
Body's mechanisms for healing	Like all cancers, it is important to get your body to recognize this area as a problem requiring your attention and focus. Your immune system and white blood cells must be alerted to the area of concern. Create more specific visualizations using previous concepts.
	 skin organ

4) Pancreatic Cancer Table

Possible causes or risk factors	• Presently there is controversy about the causes of pancreatic cancer. • Smoking increases the risk of pancreatic cancer. • Diet: Risk is increased with high intake of meat, fat and alcohol. • Environment: There is an increased risk with long-term exposure to certain chemicals, such as petroleum products and some insecticides.
Anatomy of problem area	The pancreas is an organ in the digestive system which secretes important digestive enzymes and hormones, including insulin.
Symptoms	May include back pain, jaundice, discomfort around stomach area.
Body's mechanisms for healing	Like all cancers, it is important to get your body to recognize this area as a problem requiring your attention and focus. Create more specific visualizations using previous concepts.
	 Pancreas liver stomach gallbladder pancreas

4) Prostate Cancer Table

Possible causes or risk factors	• Diet: cholesterol in the blood may accelerate the growth of prostate tumors ("Journal of Clinical Investigation", April 1, 2004) • Men over age 50 are at risk for prostate cancer and risk increases with age. • There are a number of other controversial causes which are presently being studied.
Anatomy of problem Area	Prostate is a small gland which surrounds the urethra and is located below the bladder in males. It produces the fluid in semen and can affect the flow of urine.
Symptoms	Difficulty, pain or frequent urinating. Blood may be present in urine or semen.
Body's mechanisms for healing	Like all cancers, it is important to get your body to recognize this area as a problem requiring your attention and focus. Create more specific visualizations using previous concepts.
	Prostate

5) Colorectal Cancer Table

Possible causes or risk factors	• Stress • Diet • Lifestyle habits (i.e. smoking) • Lack of exercise • Environment
Anatomy of problem area	The colon, or large intestine, extracts water and salts from feces. It consists of ascending, transverse, descending and sigmoid colon.
Symptoms	May include rectal bleeding, colon blockages, abdominal distension, nausea, vomiting.
Body's mechanisms for healing	Like all cancers, it is important to get your body to recognize this area as a problem requiring your attention and focus. Create more specific visualizations using previous concepts.

Visualize the Latest Research

Nearly every day brings news of a breakthrough in cancer esearch. There are many interesting studies that you will read about. You may even inquire about your eligibility to participate in a study. Instead of feeling disappointed if you aren't selected, visualize that you are part of the study. In your mind's eye, see yourself involved with any cutting edge research that captures your attention. Be inspired to keep up with the latest research and participate in your own way.

The easiest way for me to explain this concept of "imaginary" participation in a study is with the following example. Recently there was major network press about the "Kanzius Machine" (CBS News- "The Kanzius Machine: A Cancer Cure?" April, 2008). It is essentially a radio wave machine used to kill cancer cells. It is based on the fact that metal heats up when it is exposed to radio waves. The challenge is to inject a metallic substance specifically where the tumor is located and ensure that the metal can be safely removed from the area after the cancer has been destroyed.

Research is currently exploring the use of metallic nanoparticles which when heated by radio waves effectively destroy cancer cells. When injected directly into the tumor, the cells start falling apart as the space between cells increases. Cancer cells in the target area die and there appears to be no damage to the surrounding tissue.

Human trials are still at least four years away but you have the ability to visualize this now!

Visualizations

Radio Wave Visualization:

- *Focus your mind on the location of the tumor.*
- *Visualize injecting metallic nanoparticles directly into the tumor which are attracted to every cell in the tumor.*
- *Know that these metallic nanoparticles attract and attach like magnets to the cells of the tumor.*
- *Generate the imaginary radio waves focused on the tumor.*
- *In your mind's eye see the tumor cells absorbing the heat until they die.*
- *Once all cancer cells are dead, see them disintegrate so there is no longer any evidence of any cancer ever being there.*
- *KNOW that your intentions are influencing your healing.*

Improving Techniques for Visualizations

Check out the following techniques in my earlier books which can be used to enhance any of your visualizations. In " *DreamHealer 2- Guide to Self-Empowerment,*" there are exercises to increase your sensitivity to subtle energies, including seeing and feeling the energy. My third book, *"The Path of the DreamHealer,"* details the technique of combing your energy and talking to your cells to get them all vibrating in unison. My DVD, *"Visualizations for Self-Empowerment,"* contains many helpful visualizations which can be integrated into your healing process. Since these techniques are not repeated in *"Intention Heals,"* you should check out this information to receive the maximum benefit for your healing journey. Remember that visualizations can be used in conjunction with any other treatment.

Integrate your visualizations into your everyday life, as a routine. Change them and mix it up so that you look forward to doing them. This should be an enjoyable experience as brain stimulating exercises are more effective if you are motivated. That is the point of customizing; to make your visualizations *fun, stimulating* and *meaningful to you*.

Rely on your memory of what you loved or create a memory from what you want to do and rehearse it as if it were taking place. Use ideas from your *intention chart* to make visualizing comfortable, realistic and automatic. Know that you perceive your world in a way which is most meaningful and helpful to you and change your reality to what you need it to be.

Visualizations

Visualization may be a new skill for you, so be patient as change takes time to integrate it into your life. Doing visualizations before bedtime creates optimum conditions for change, as you set your intentions and align conscious visualizations with subconscious sleep in your imaginative state. Another optimum condition is the meditative state when the conscious self does not override your creative capacity for change.

Change the pattern of your past, as this changes your present and future. Unlearn a negative pattern by replacing it with a positive one. Doing visualizations strengthen neural pathways and connections which are beneficial to you. Visualizations are mental exercises to harness the power of your intentions.

"We perceive our reality in a way which most closely meets our needs. Therefore, our world is what we have asked it to be."
- Adam

Visualizations Summary

Change or customize the visualization to suit you. Visualizations are a tool for you to use. Your response to them is a very individual process and so is what works most effectively for you.

Ask yourself the following questions:

1. *Have I researched my area of concern thoroughly enough to create accurate visualizations?*
2. *Do I understand the body's mechanisms for healing this area?*
3. *Do I know what the proper and healthy functioning of this area should be?*
4. *Have I practiced anatomically accurate visualizations, or varied general ones according to my specific challenge?*
5. *Have I modified the specific visualizations which are most relevant for me and customized them according to my experiences in life?*

All of the visualizations in this book are designed to make you feel more comfortable as you explore and practice what works most effectively for you. TRY IT!! Becoming comfortable with yourself is the most important step toward self-empowerment. Trust yourself on your way forward!

This is what healing with intentions is all about.
Practice makes perfect!
You now have the tools.
It's up to you.
Enjoy the journey!

Healing Visualizations

The following visualizations are just a few of the thousands I have received by email and letter. These customized visualization techniques come from individuals who have read the *"DreamHealer"* books, seen the DVD and/or have attended my workshops. It is inspiring for me to hear how people are creatively using visualization techniques to address their particular health challenges. As you will see, they have adapted the basic principles of visualization and made them meaningful in their own healing. I hope these will inspire you and provide motivation as you develop your own unique visualizations to improve your health.

General visualization

I think it's important to wake up each day smiling and keep a smile all day! Smile and the world will smile with you! Whatever you are visualizing - Make sure that you are "SMILING" the whole time. A smile goes to the core of your being and this is what you need to make it manifest changes.

General visualization

I visualize cell level breathing as I breathe in and expand the light deep into my skeleton and all my body's cells. Then I flush negative patterning that is most often imprinted by the time we are five years old. This has helped me a great deal in stepping into my power.

181

General visualization

I think about the sky on a very clear night. I visualize that I breathe into my being the moon, the stars, the shooting stars, the comets, the little dipper and the big dipper . I then visualize the little dipper pouring the stars and shooting stars down my pipes, my valves, my tubes, my arteries and veins. At the other end I have the Big Dipper picking up all the yuck that has been forced out of my pipes by the force of the stars and shooting stars. I am now clean of negative substances in my body.

General visualization

When I'm sick or intuitively feel as though something is "off" I get into the shower. As it's cascading down on my head I visualize color instead of water coming down through my crown chakra, down through all the chakras and spreading throughout my body. Then I see whatever it is that is negative flowing out of my body and down the drain of the shower.

General visualization

Your books have inspired me to be a catalyst for my own healing…and never lose hope. Already I am experiencing increased vitality in body, mind and spirit and feel awakened to the reverence and intelligence of all life in each moment. God bless you in assisting so many millions of people to become self-healers.

Addictions

I use light to open up and clean off dopamine receptors in my brain. Then I release a shot of dopamine and a shot of the enzyme that controls my brain's reaction to the dopamine. By co-releasing the enzyme which is usually restricted by the drug's hi-jacking of the receptors and transmitters, my brain reacts in a more normal manner to dopamine.

By knowing my abuse pattern, I regulate my dopamine distribution and return it to a more normal level, taking away the imbalance which creates the overwhelming appetite for the drug. After regular treatments of two to three weeks, I am over my extreme cravings.

Alopecia

Thanks for your inspirational work! I had alopecia and was told by many dermatologists that there was no chance I would ever have any hair regrowth. Since I have read your books and attended several workshops, I now have a mane! I visualize wavy, thick hair growing and it is happening! My hair is continuing to grow. Thank you!

Alzheimer's

I have been diagnosed with early stage Alzheimer's. I use the lightning bolt visualizations together with vivid memories of energy and finish with the waterfall. I find my memory improves when pinching out the lightning bolts using my energetic finger nails (Bear claws). Wow! Good luck with your studies at University.

Arthritis

When I do my visualization on my slightly swollen finger joint, I visualize white flakes of arthritis gently floating out and fading into the air.

Bells Palsy

I use Adam's suggestion of lightning bolts entering my body from the top of my head, especially on the right side of my face and back of my head. I do my visualizations at a quiet time during my day. I also try to do them at night right before I go to sleep.

Cancer

I visualize a small vacuum cleaner, sucking disease out of every corner.

Assisting with Chemotherapy

I am undergoing chemotherapy and will have radiation. I visualize molecules of the chemotherapy as silver molecules like ball bearings running through the liquid drug. The molecules stick together as strings and are able to surround the cancer cells and alienate them so they cannot communicate. Then I imagine they are able to annihilate the cancer cells by exploding and vaporizing the cancer cells. Afterwards I imagine a blue angel pouring blue water into my body through my head to repair the damage to my body.

Visualizations

Bladder Cancer

I imagine millions of fizzing, healing, bubbles as you would see when you pour a bottle of soda in a glass. I feel this fizzing action where my pain is. I feel the fizzing dissolve my pain and bring healing oxygen to my body. I use this to heal my cancer. Last July I was diagnosed with stage 4 bladder cancer and was not expected to live for more than a few months. After using this visualization every day and night, the doctors were surprised to find a significant improvement in my health. Since then I haven't needed any chemo or any drugs whatsoever. I continue to use this visualization often and now the cancer is almost gone.

Breast Cancer

My mantra (or my talk to myself) when I feel fear or any other emotion I do not need. I am happy, I am healthy, I am holy. It reminds me that I am a part of something much bigger and that I am a joyful person at heart and that I am indeed healthy! I "SEE" myself Happy and Healthy and what I "SEE" today, I will become tomorrow!

Leukemia

I visualize lightning striking my bone marrow. I see this as God's healing energy, filled with complete love, being directed into the marrow of my bones. This includes thanking the leukemia cells for getting my attention and letting them know I do not need them any longer and they must leave. The lightning is now filling my bone marrow with complete healthy blood cells that are able to do their perfect purpose. This 'lightning' is also balancing all cells in my bone marrow for my optimum health.

185

Lung Cancer

I bought Adam's DVD and initially focused on Fire, Cancer, Lungs, Emotions and Waterfall visualizations. I spent five minutes on each followed by good intentions for the day. Once I received the news that my CT scan was clear of tumors, I then focused on Fire, Lungs, Emotions and Waterfall visualizations with the same five minutes followed by good intentions. I do this work in my office at my computer station.

Multiple Myeloma

When I first met you five years ago I had multiple myeloma, from which I was not expected to recover. I recently saw my second opinion doctor and he was surprised to see me after 5 years. He could not believe my blood test results and the fact that after 5 years there was NO SIGN of any multiple myeloma. He kept saying to me that this was so rare, so unusual indeed; he wanted to know exactly what I was doing, so I told him about your books and workshops. I was sorry to miss the recent workshop of Adam's but I was cycling all weekend. Thank you Adam for sharing your gift!

Chemical Sensitivities

I have chemical sensitivities and am thrilled to report that I am doing much better by doing visualizations after attending two workshops and reading your books/DVD. I visualize that I am surrounded by all of the chemicals that I am usually reacting to, yet my cells remain relaxed. Every cell in every organ is relaxed. I imagine my organs filtering out all of the toxins, yet my cells remain relaxed, calm and completely unaffected. It works! Thank you, Adam.

Chronic Fatigue Syndrome

I begin each session with the inner statement that "I create my own reality and in this reality….." followed by the individual statements "I create a completely healthy heart & circulatory system, a completely healthy brain & neurological system." As I address each system, I see it "ablaze" with white light.

Crohn's Disease

Yesterday my family attended your workshop for the second time. My primary motivation had been to thank you in person for your healing workshop a year ago which cured my son of a twelve year struggle with Crohn's disease. He is healed completely and symptom free ever since. What I didn't anticipate was the effect of yesterday's healing on me!

Depression

I imagine that I am made completely from light. Then I imagine myself standing high upon a ridge, looking proud and confident, at peace with myself and the world below. I see myself growing brighter and brighter until I am completely white with the light. I imagine that I can see the darkness leaving my body and being returned to the sun to be transferred back into positive energy. I see myself laughing and enjoying the company of loved ones, dancing, singing, etc.
I repeat this several times a day.

Fat Burner

I really like the visualization you offered in the latest newsletter-about the mitochondria eating fat cells. I have gone one better and started singing a little song about how my mitochondria are eating all my fat cells...and when I do that, I get CONFIRMATION CHILLS!

Fibromyalgia

Whenever I'm in pain (from fibromyalgia), I lie down and start slow deep breathing, filling my lungs so they expand. Then in exhaling, I visualize energy surging toward the site of my pain. Sometimes, I can actually feel heat or tingling at the pain site. That's when I know it's working.

Thanks for spreading the truth about how we can heal ourselves. I am still fibromyalgia symptom free after 3 years, thanks to you and your sharing of teachings. With my Reiki clients, I tell them of my healing and advise them of your books and your visualizations for healing.

Gastric Problems

I surround my stomach and mid-section with a green glowing light. I do my visualizations at a quiet time during my day. I also try to do them at night right before I go to sleep. Finally, I say the mantra; "I can get well. I will be well. I am well." I say this as many times as possible each day and especially during the times when I am thinking about my health problems.

Hashimoto's Disease

I have always felt that my body was capable of healing this imbalance in my system. So I am overjoyed that after nearly two years, my blood tests show me on the low side of normal. I continue to do a visualization of my entire endocrine system working like a fine Swiss clock mechanism.

Heart

I attended your workshop yesterday as I have an enlarged left ventricle, low ejection fraction and mild heart failure. While driving to your workshop I experienced my usual shortness of breath and heart palpitations/arrhythmia. Right after your energy treatments, I was able to take full, deep, effortless inhalations for the first time in almost a year! Now I am home and have NO shortness of breath, even with brisk paced walks. I can only attribute these things to your workshop and cannot thank you enough. I look forward to seeing you at your next workshop!

Heart

I will never forget you, Adam and the healing joy that you have brought into my life. I am a Reiki Master practitioner and now have a very full life helping people. I also work at one of the private hospitals with a very famous American cardiovascular surgeon. This is going to be an exciting year for us using your visualizations and breathing techniques for healing. We are teaching medical doctors about your healing methods.

Hypertension

I use blue light around my whole body and around the heart. I do my visualizations just before I go to sleep.

Memory

The visualization technique that I find most helpful is the one that descends like a bolt of lightning. I stop it in the head where it tumbles around to realign faulty wiring that causes defects in memory and impedes mental clarity. I do this in the morning at the time of my usual meditation and find it helpful.

Multiple Sclerosis

I relax and get comfortable. I imagine, at arms length above my head, a gold color that falls around my body like an egg shell shape, finishing under my feet. I then imagine using a soft large paint brush. I dip the brush in a gold, loving light and paint it on any area where I have pain or a problem, emotional or physical, then relax about 20 minutes. This has helped me to fill up every cell with light and allow the shadows and dull areas to be transformed. It really works for my MS.

Multiple Sclerosis

I knit myelin around my nerves. Then I stretch out my nerves and wrap them with a myelin ribbon.

Multiple Sclerosis

I regenerate tissue- the myelin sheath surrounding the nerves. I knit material and coat the fibers by weaving an ever denser material where needed. In order to get the raw materials to where they are needed, I inject light energy directly into the area I am working on and solidify it with beams of intense light.

Muscles

This visualization was inspired by your sets of visualizations on your DVD and also by a particular scene in one of the Harry Potter movies. First I visualize the shape of the bicep muscle and start freezing it with a gradual freeze (as in the frozen lake scene where Harry Potter is lying on the ground with his father). I see the muscle gradually being covered by the white freezing snow and then see the whole muscle frozen (as in frozen meat). I hold the visualization for a little while and then I proceed to see it thaw gradually until it is red and healthy. I continue the visualization by lifting the muscle off the bone using my two hands side by side and grabbing the muscle (This move is taken from an actual move in Indian Head Massage.) Then I release the muscle. I usually do this visualization two or three times in one session.

Pain

I am lying down on a blanket on a nice green lawn, with no chance of anyone or anything disturbing my privacy. It is a lovely warm day and the sun is not in my eyes. There is a little breeze and I am in a comfortable position. My arms are out to my sides and my palms are face up. I look up at the sky and a very beautiful silver cloud begins to drift through the sky until it is directly over me. It stops and begins to shimmer and grow brighter. Then it gently releases a mist of white that sparkles like diamonds and it falls all over my body. It especially heaps up onto my painful area which begins to feel warm and very cozy. A sweet, soft voice is whispering into my ear, telling me that I am being healed of this pain.

Relaxation

My cells receive and transmit emotion in the form of light so I imagine the calmest frame of mind I can. I imagine that I project this into my cells. My cells recognize this emotional input as being different than just light on its own and this will bring a more intense form of relief than just light by itself. Then, as beautiful, calm emotion is administered directly into my brain, I often drift into a deep sleep.

Sleep

I visualize myself in a healing bath when I go to sleep at night. I visualize healing bubbles surrounding my body and energy going into my cells. My muscles actually start to twitch and if I am not careful I get too energized to go to sleep! Wonderful stuff!! Before falling asleep every night, I lie in bed on my back, feet 2-3 feet apart, arms and hands flat beside me.

With each inhale I visualize white healing light drawing up from my toes progressively through my entire body. With each exhale, I expel the unhealthy/negatives that the white light is healing and replacing. When I feel/see a break or slow-down in the flow of white light, then I know I have to stop and concentrate on that particular area before I can continue. The light travels from my toes, up to knees, to hips and through each internal organ, up through my shoulders. The light then meets the light that has come up from my fingertips to arms, up my neck and fills my head. When I exhale only 'white smoke', I fall into a deep, healing sleep.

Sleep

I want to share my experience of being guided. I had the sensation of being submerged in a deep blue, effervescent pool of liquid. Messages seemed to flood through me resulting in a whole -body rhythmic pulsing sensation, with a bright white heat radiating from my face. With these sensations came instructions on how to cure my insomnia, explaining that my thoughts are energy. I became aware that my energy jams up in loops and gets fragmented which keeps me awake until dawn trying to decipher it. The cure is a visualization: breathing in a relaxed way and exhaling out a smoky stream of jumbled thoughts. My sleep has become the deepest and most restful I can ever remember. So, once again, Adam, my profound, humble and eternal gratitude.

Smoking

I locate an area in my DNA where the false message of the need to smoke is indicated by a blinking light. After that, I imagine taking a small pair of golden tweezers in one hand and extracting that message out. At the same time, I hold a laser in my other hand and through beaming the light into the area with the new message: "I am a non smoker" or "I have lost my desire for tobacco in any form" to be now inserted and welded into that area where the old message of being a smoker once was.

Spine

I visualize my spine at the core of my body with my cerebrospinal fluid inside it. I imagine that this fluid is divine in essence. It is silky, velvety, glowing silver. Then I imagine that this silver radiance is spreading and expanding to fill my entire body. I allow this to fill my head and spread into my chest, heart and head. It bathes my sinuses and nourishes my brain. I let it branch into my arms and hands. It fills my abdomen and digestive organs, so I am soaking in silver radiance created from my core. I let it fill me from head to toe until my entire body is a glowing silver that nourishes me. I am soaking in silver radiance created from my core.

Stroke

I put together scanned pictures from your books in my healing book, so I always have a visual aid to do my visualizing to heal my body from a stroke and diabetes. I see myself in the form of a hologram in front of me, with total health information inside. Then I focus on visualizing white blood cells clearing up any damaged areas from my stroke. I see bolts of white light rebooting my left shoulder, arm, wrist, hand and fingers, foot, ankle, leg and hip, allowing total freedom of movement without pain or discomfort. I see resetting my left side totally to my desired wellness and move with ease.

Virus

I imagine that the light is a bug zapper operating similar to the type used for killing outdoor insects. I see a single virus evaporating as it is zapped by the light and it turns to dust. Then I imagine seeing thousands of them being zapped by the light. I repeat this and each time I imagine that their numbers are diminishing, as there are fewer left to kill. I visualize that the dust left behind is being removed through my kidneys. I see and know that I have destroyed them all and my body is clear.

Spirituality

I am a Haida woman and have witnessed in our community the sadness, loss and grief that manifests in physical ailments- mainly heart disease, diabetes and addictions (alcohol, drugs, food and cigarettes). I feel that the ONE thing that my people need is to regain this empowerment of self that you help to teach. Our people have "lost" that ability through governmental systems, residential schools, sexual, physical and spiritual abuse. I have attended your workshop and watched your DVD and read your books. I will now be taking back some of the control in my life and will share this with others in our community. Thank you for being inspirational.

Spirituality

Many of the beliefs that you shared at the conference are those of the First Nations people. Our people are very spiritual. When I met you, words couldn't describe how I felt inside. I just wanted to cry and it was hard for me to even speak. It was like seeing someone I lost a long time ago and finally found that person. Seeing what I saw, hearing what I heard, feeling what I felt is an experience I will never forget. A day never goes by when you are not on my mind. You have triggered the return of many thoughts of my teachings from Elders, Medicine men and Healers. Adam, you have helped me to remember who I am, where I come from and how fortunate that I am to have so many special people in my life. I just want to thank you from the bottom of my heart and soul.

Spirituality

Your books have helped me tremendously as you really have a way of making difficult things easy to comprehend. I am a Bible scholar and find it interesting that everything you teach is in accord with the scripture. You teach a lot about quantum physics which is your foundation for energy healing. This makes sense to me and my belief in "God." In fact, God used your books to help me to see how "He" works in one area as well as in another area at the same time; because ALL is God.

"What appears to separate us
is only illusionary.
It follows that what we do for ourselves
is ultimately what we do for everyone.
Helping everyone is therefore
an unavoidable outcome of
truly helping ourselves."
- Adam.

***

If you would like to share your creative visualizations
or testimonials, please email your information to:
visualizations@dreamhealer.com

Good luck on your healing journey and I hope this book has been an inspiration to awaken the healer within you.

Stay Tuned!!!

<u>Notes</u>

About the Author

*Adam is an internationally renowned energy healer, best-selling author and speaker. He combines his First Nations (Native American) healing background with channelled insights and academic background in Molecular Biology. Aware of his ability to influence health, he has dedicated himself to teaching self-empowerment techniques, enabling others to access their own innate healing abilities. His focus is bridging cutting edge science with our intuitive abilities to heal thus.... **INTENTION HEALS.***